Andreas Lommel · SHAMANISM: The Beginnings of Art

Andreas Lommel

SHAMANISM
The beginnings of art

McGRAW-HILL BOOK COMPANY
New York · Toronto

Translated from the German by Michael Bullock

709.01
L 84∿

CONTENTS

INTRODUCTION

Because their world is represented today by only a few small remnants of dwindling human groups, there is a need for an intensive study of the early hunters of the Stone Age, their life and ideas, their way of thinking and their art.

Hunters who still live today as they were living 10000 years ago are now to be found only in the northernmost regions of the earth: these are the well-known Eskimos. A few other groups have been preserved in Southern Africa, Australia, and South America, and there are a few infinitesimal remnants in South-East Asia.

When we recall that all great civilizations, including our own, are based on agriculture, it at once becomes clear that the hunters represent an earlier stage of human culture, the one preceding agriculture. Thus the groups that still exist present the only opportunity for studying a highly interesting stage of cultural development dating from the earliest times.

The central figure among hunters is the shaman, the magician-priest, medicine man, doctor, who even today is still to be found almost everywhere among the extant groups. This interesting figure is by no means merely a conjurer or charlatan.

The interest of the general public in the now-vanished world of the early hunters, their way of thinking, and the phenomenon of shamanism was first aroused by Rasmussen with his book *Thulefahrt*[1] in 1926. Without himself advancing detailed theories or explanations of shamanism, he allows his Eskimo informants to speak. The simple and impressive language of these men retains its vivid quality through all translations.

Numerous Russian and American anthropologists have studied living hunting peoples in Siberia and North America and have tried to penetrate their mental life. These investigators have employed the scientific methods of ethnology and sociology in their study of the hunting peoples—but where the problems of shamanism are concerned this approach is inadequate. Here the findings of modern psychology must also be brought to bear.

Shamanism as an attitude of mind is first and foremost a psychological problem. Naturally shamanism is also a cultural, historical, and ethnological phenomenon, but its psychological side must not be overlooked.

If we look upon shamanism not as a form of religion—as was usual up to now—but more as a complex of religious notions and modes of behaviour, we are then faced with the question of the personality of the shaman.

The anthropologist Ursula Knoll-Greiling wrote a book devoted to an examination of the psychic structure of the shaman's personality and reached important conclusions.[2] She discovered that certain shamanistic phenomena correspond to the modern definitions of certain mental disorders.

The questions she posed regarding the shaman's personality structure will be taken up again in the following study and pursued further on the basis of the material which she assembled. Naturally, in investigating shamanism we must not stop at the pathological phenomena, at the definition of certain mental disorders: the most important thing about the shaman is that by means of a therapeutic process which we cannot yet understand or explain he is able to cure mental disorders. Precisely this ability to cure himself and progress from, let us say, a 'negative' psychological state to a 'positive' and productive one constitutes the difference between him and the modern psychotic. We shall find that a study of the shaman as an artistically productive personality leads to far-reaching discoveries on the one hand regarding the artistic personality as such, and on the other regarding the whole history of early art.

In order to study the psychology of shamanism we must, of course, also take account of the art of shamanism. Curiously enough, up to now this has been done only to a very limited extent, and above all investigators have fought shy of connecting early Stone Age art with shamanism and explaining it by shamanistic ideas. But it seems entirely possible to link very early rupestrian art, such as the Ice Age paintings of southern France and northern Spain, with shamanism by the study of particular motifs that are related to shamanism. It is true that such an attempt cannot solve the riddle of the quality of early rock-paintings, but it can lead to what we may call an iconographic understanding of this art.

We can still follow various motifs that occur in the rock-paintings almost down to our own day, where they lead an insignificant existence in a more simplified form in the everyday decorative art of the hunting peoples. But we can also link up these motifs with the myths and from this point reach a far-reaching interpretation of the early rock-paintings.

The shaman is not merely a medicine man, a doctor or a man with priestly functions, he is above all an artistically productive man, in the truest sense of the word creative—in fact, he is probably the first artistically active man known to us. In order to understand him it is not enough merely to explain his significance in terms of the history of civilization, or to interpret it psychologically; we must also consider his position and his nature as an artist. From this standpoint we shall then be able to gain insights into the nature of prehistoric art and to understand the Ice Age artist, the man who painted the pictures on the cave walls at Lascaux and Altamira.

In investigating shamanism we must disregard the many later accretions that were taken over in the course of time by the highly developed civilizations and go back, as it were, to the primordial form or quintessence of shamanism. It would be wrong to look upon this term as only being justified by the latter accretions. For example, iron

Shaman beating a drum: modern Eskimo drawing

plays an enormous role in Siberian shamanism, but must be a later accretion; shamanism without the whole complex of iron is conceivable and indeed demonstrable.

For a start we need to establish as precise a definition as possible of the term 'shamanism.' Although everyone will connect with the term shamanism a more or less definite notion which is largely correct and in accordance with the facts, only few will be clear about the demarcation line between the terms shaman and medicine man, about the mutual relationship between the two institutions.

Even in the scientific literature only an extremely inexact distinction between the two terms is made right up to the present. This fact is easily understood when we know that among primitive peoples 'shaman' and 'medicine man' mean very largely the same, perform the same functions and employ the same psychological technique. But the medicine man and the shaman have quite different personalities, and the psychological preconditions are quite different in each case, even if the function of the two and their significance for the psychic constitution of the particular primitive group may be very similar.

It is well known that medicine men occur in almost all primitive human groups. The medicine man is first and foremost the doctor, but he almost always occupies a central position within the group. Often he is the antipode of the chief; sometimes both functions are assumed by one person, and for the most part his role goes beyond that of the doctor and approaches that of the spiritual guide and priest or even of the modern psychologist. As a personality the medicine man is usually of preeminent intelligence and possessed of a definite power urge.

The capacities of the medicine man—in addition to simple conjuring tricks and perhaps solid medical ability—consist above all in a gift for suggestion and hypnosis. Somehow he acquires through his training the ability to influence his fellow tribesmen.

Suggestion provides the ultimate explanation for almost all the 'miracles' worked by medicine men, such as telepathic phenomena, clairvoyance, dream journeys, mysterious disappearance and reappearance, and the like.

Drawing of a spirit by an Eskimo. The spirit's mute eeriness had such an effect on the artist that he fled without having taken it as his helping spirit

The difference between medicine men and shamans lies on the one hand in the differing form and intensity with which the 'call' is experienced, and on the other in the different technique employed for influencing people.

Unlike the medicine man, the future shaman acts under an inner compulsion. In many cases, as is frequently and clearly expressed in Siberian reports, the young man who is seized and oppressed by the 'spirits' has absolutely no wish to become a shaman, but sees no other way out.

Translating this into modern terms intelligible to us, a psychosis that is emerging for some reason or other is so strong that the only way out open to the individual attacked by it is to escape from it into shamanistic activity, that is to say essentially by means of artistic productivity, dancing, singing, etc.

The position of the shaman is outwardly very similar to that of the medicine man, and in many cases the two cannot be distinguished. The shaman also exercises the functions of priest, spiritual guide, and doctor. In contradistinction to the medicine man, however, he always acts in a state of trance into which he puts himself. His conjurations of the spirits, his therapeutic efforts are never carried out by him in a state of clear consciousness but always in one of rapt trance. In accordance with this, psychic phenomena, such as telepathy, clairvoyance, mysterious disappearance and reappearance, always predominate among the shaman's activities. Whereas in the case of the medicine man such abilities fall more within the sphere of conjuring performed to reinforce the suggestive effect on the audience, the shaman experiences all psycho-logical phenomena with great intensity in himself.

Whereas in the case of the medicine man a striving for power is clearly discernible, the shaman is a more complex personality. Very often it was not his wish to become a shaman, but he was forced into this path by a particular experience, the experience of being 'called'. It is true that the shaman exercises a great influence on his environment and his social function is undoubtedly that of supervising and maintaining the psycho-logical equilibrium of his community. He does not acquire this social function as the result of striving for power, however, but as the outcome of his own psychological development. Only to a superficial observer, therefore, are the abilities and functions of the two largely the same. The psychological differences between medicine man and shaman lie in the totally different evolution which leads each of them to his calling, the totally different personality structure and inner attitude to the community, in the different technique for influencing the community and in the shaman's often consider-able artistic achievement as singer, dancer, painter, and theatrical producer, which the medicine man lacks.

An investigation of this figure among various peoples or groups, through various epochs, therefore promises exceptional insights into the nature of the human mind, its manifestations, and its activities. For a start we must define the term shamanism more precisely. To shamanize means to render 'the spirits' subservient to oneself.

The spirits are inner images, ideas of a personal or collective kind that have taken on form, images from the mythology of the tribe, of the group, very old traditional ideas, the whole complex of beliefs belonging to the so-called 'animal level'.

The shaman gives these images shape by portraying them and identifying himself with them, recognizing and using them as real forces, interpreting them artistically. Shamanizing seems to be that psychic technique by means of which one can subordinate 'the spirits' to oneself; that is to say, bring order into one's own chaotic psyche and gain control of the power of one's own unconscious imagery. This seems only to be possible in an ever-repeated state of trance.

As a rule the literature on shamanism confines itself almost exclusively to reports from Siberia and North America. But the phenomenon of shamanism must be granted a far wider distribution. Shamanism seems to occur in almost every area where an early hunting economy has continued virtually to our own day; that is to say, in Siberia, North America, South America, various regions of Africa, and also in certain zones of Australia. In Siberia and North America we see shamanistic phenomena in a pure form; in the other regions named we have to distinguish the shamanistic pheno-mena from the activities of the medicine man, as we often can. In Australia, for example, shamanism seems to occur above all on the north-western periphery of the continent, whereas the 'medicine men', who are to be found everywhere else, display shamanistic features only to a limited degree.[3]

Without doubt, the shaman also exercises the functions of a medicine man, but he goes beyond this. Above all, however, he comes into being through quite different preconditions, his intellectual and psychological attitude is quite different from that of a medicine man or sorcerer. In the true sense, therefore, that man alone becomes a shaman who is chosen and called for this vocation by 'the spirits'. The 'spirits' take possession of a man, force him into madness and sickness. He either perishes under this coercion or he frees himself from it by beginning to 'shamanize'.

The 'spirits' are, of course, not spiritual beings existing outside man and influencing him, taking possession of him, etc., but a man's own ideas, images of his own psyche, manifestations of his own ego.

In primitive man these mental images are overwhelmingly powerful, and so long as they remain unordered and unrestrained they can destroy him, can drive him to madness.

Through lack of objectivity to himself primitive man, or the man 'possessed' in the case of an overpowerful manifestation, is not capable of recognizing the 'spirits' as phenomena originating from his own psyche: they appear to him to be beings from another world that are taking possession of him.

It is above all the activation of the powers of unconscious imagery which evoke and constitute the healing process. During the initiation period and then during the shaman-istic performance 'the shaman speaks with spirits'. The spirits very often come to him in the shape of animals, so he can describe them and portray them in pictures, masks and dramatic actions.

A creative component in the personality of the shaman becomes active, which enables him to overcome his pathological predisposition.

The essential factor in his experience of being called is the demand made upon him to become artistically creative.

Shamanism is therefore a mental attitude that comes into being through the over-coming of a mental illness.

Unlike the medicine man, the shaman's adoption of his profession is in many cases not voluntary. The future shaman's experience of being called seems frequently to consist in a compulsive state from which he sees no other means of escape than to 'shamanize'. It is often clear, particularly from reports from Siberia, that the man who is to become a shaman consciously does not wish to do so at all, but is driven and forced to it by the 'spirits', and finally, in order not to perish, takes the only path open to him and becomes a shaman.

The future shaman, the young man suited for shamanizing, is a sick man. He suffers from psychopathic or epileptic states and is very often also physically ill. He cannot escape the demands of the spirits, which drive him deeper and deeper into the illness, although he very often tries to resist. He gets into a situation, into a mental illness, from which he can find no way out but death or the assumption of the office of shaman.

Part of the shaman's activity consists in the trance. During initiation and during artistic creation the essential thing for the shaman is a displacement of the plane of consciousness. Clear consciousness is eliminated. Images are activated on another plane of consciousness. These images are always taken from the world-view, mythology, and

The melancholy helping spirit Isitoq or Giant-Eye. He has thick, coarse hair that stands on end; each eye is divided into two compartments and the large mouth is placed vertically, with one long tooth at the top and two shorter ones at the side. His speciality is finding people who have broken the taboo

religion of the tribe or culture group in question. But instead of these images being given form in a conscious state, this takes place in an unconscious or subconscious state. The shaman sings, dances, mimes—he may even paint and draw in a trance, from which he then awakes. Once awake he often no longer remembers, or remembers only dimly, his actions while in the trance. If the calling to be a shaman may be described as a kind of self-cure of a profound psychosis, 'shamanizing' consists in a repetition of this healing process.

In the shaman's trance not only is the collective psyche brought into order and the tribal community filled with new confidence in their luck at hunting or the like; a way is also shown by means of which certain psychoses rife in the particular group may be overcome.

Since shamanism is predominantly and most clearly observed in the subarctic regions, investigators have spoken of an 'arctic madness', a kind of psychosis which is perhaps caused by the extraordinarily difficult climatic conditions in the subarctic landscape.

Typical of the shaman, in any case, is the repeated inducement of a state of trance, the experience of being called, the continual reactivation of the images of the tribe's mythology, considerable artistic activity, the self-cure of a psychosis through this activity, and therapeutic activity performed in a state of trance. Only where these features are present can we speak of shamanism; all other similar activities should be described as the functions of a medicine man.

Whether the practices of the medicine man are derived from shamanism and are, as it were, a diluted infusion of shamanism, which is itself confined to cultures based on hunting, or whether shamanism is a particularly intensified form of the practices of the medicine man is a question that cannot be decided here.

We must note that part of the definition of shamanism lies in the self-cure of a deep depression by the use of a certain psychic technique.

The technique consists in the sufferer's setting himself in a trance or trancelike state by means of monotonous sounds, drumbeats, and dancing. In this state consciousness is eliminated and images are taken over from the subconscious. These images may be of all kinds, but are always drawn from the mythological notions and world-view of the tribe concerned.

Apart from healing the sick, the shaman's social function consists above all in bringing psychic calm and confidence to the tribal community by revitalizing and intensifying its notions of the world. This is particularly the meaning of the annual hunting rites carried out by the shaman.

To be a successful shaman requires a specific predisposition that is universal. The shaman must be artistically gifted and possess a talent for improvisation, for quickly adapting himself to any given situation. For he often has to make statements on the spur of the moment regarding the weather, sickness, war, and so on, frequently even in a poetic and sometimes even in a rhythmically musical form, in order to render his state-ments more impressive and intensify their effect on his listeners. Furthermore, it is to be assumed that shamans are good psychologists who know intuitively how to create a suitable atmosphere of tension and receptiveness among their audience. Evidently only men of many gifts and exceptional qualities are suited to this profession.

This predisposition is, however, also manifested in certain peculiarities. The future shaman stands apart from the community and attracts attention by a curious attitude to his environment.

Very frequently the peculiarity of the shamanistic temperament is also manifested in occasional abnormal states that may exhibit hysteroid or schizoid forms. Even attacks of paralysis are not rare in this connexion. Looked at from the modern viewpoint the shamanistic disposition may have a psychopathological aspect.[4] But this aspect alone is not enough. It is undoubtedly present, but the essential thing is the capacity for the cure, and indeed the self-cure of the unstable shamanistic personality. This is not done by one single cure; the healing process must be undertaken again and again.

Again and again the shaman has to free himself from a deep depression by a creative act. By action he has to bind the disintegrating elements of his psyche into a unity by means of a synthesis, a mysterious psychic activity.

The personality structure of the shaman seems to be very similar in all the regions where shamanism occurs. We should hardly credit a 'primitive society' with the ability to produce such a complex personality, and above all with the capacity of this person-ality to react with such brilliant efficacy to its own mental disorder.

Primitive man must at a very early stage have understood and utilized certain struc-tures and potentialities of the human psyche, and above all have recognized and developed the possibility of curing mental disorders.

Self-portrait of the shaman Arnaqaoq

THE DEVELOPMENT OF THE SHAMAN

Shamanism and the hunting community

Ethnology divides human cultures into two major groups: hunters and planters.

The hunting cultures, which are still to be found today in rudimentary shape, represent an early form. The planting cultures are the later form: are, in fact, the basis of modern civilization.

The world-view or feeling for life of the two cultures is fundamentally different. The planter has a certain idea of how he can render his environment useful. He carries on a productive economy, and his aim is to multiply his possessions. The hunter hunts and seizes what he finds. He feels himself one with nature and does not wish to dominate it in the modern sense; but as a hunter he kills the animal, and this murder which is necessary to his existence gradually comes to weigh heavily upon him. It seems as though one of early man's most important tasks is to free himself from this burden. He abolishes death in his imagination. The early hunter invents the immortal soul and eternal life, in order to be able to say that he does not really kill the animals but only their bodies, and that, if their bones are rightly treated, the animals can rise again from them. This conception, this attempt at an excuse, then leads on to concepts or notions of a world beyond, to which the souls of slain animals return and from which they come forth again—from which, by appropriate means, they can be enticed. The shaman—or more precisely his soul—can visit this 'land' and cause animals, animal souls, to come to men, so that hunger and want are avoided. Hence the world these people imagine is one animated by spirits and souls, and out of it arises a truly spiritual conception of the world.

It is, of course, surprising to discover that early man, the Stone Age hunter, must have been a spiritual man—that is to say, not a 'primitive' in the sense in which we have been accustomed to picture him.

This man is primitive in the true sense of the word only in so far as he represents a beginning of human development, but not in the sense that he was an intellectually limited being, a kind of half-animal—as he is portrayed in the dermatoplastic reconstructions based on early skulls and used to illustrate popular books.

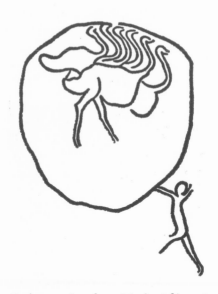

Rock-engraving from North Africa. An ostrich hunter. What is depicted is probably not a hunting implement but hunting magic

Naturally it is difficult for modern man to do justice to early man and his intellectual activity. But a study of shamanism, and above all of the art of shamanism, that is to say of the early rock-paintings, should make it possible for us to find a path to the understanding of early man.

No one denies that the rock-paintings are a unique and transcendent art, but there is still great reluctance to admit that the artists who created this art must also have been men of unique intellectual greatness. Their capacity to express themselves artistically must have corresponded to an intellectual activity that was just as unique and evolved as the art.

The art that testifies to this intellectual activity is still visible to us today—the intellectual activity itself, the world-picture and ideas, the religion, the philosophy of these men, must be laboriously deduced from the residue of ideas that has been preserved among the still living hunting peoples. It is true that the hunting peoples of our own day represent a remnant of prehistoric hunting cultures, but they have been radically changed by the influence exerted on them by various civilizations.

No firm deductions regarding earlier times can any longer be made from the hunting practices of modern man, even if certain customs go back a very long way.

It is true that in the course of time hunting has concentrated more and more on the use of complicated apparatus, but a path leads naturally from the modern telescopic sight via medieval hunting with crossbow and nets to primitive hunting with pitfalls. If we follow this path farther, we can clearly see that in the beginning of hunting a minimum of apparatus was very probably counterbalanced by a maximum of knowledge, concentration, and the gift of empathy, just as nowadays a minimum of knowledge and concentration is counterbalanced by maximum technical perfection of the weapons.

At a very early stage hunters employed a degree of ingenuity in the invention of techniques and instruments with which we should never have credited such 'primitive' people. Think of weapons like the bow and arrow, the boomerang or harpoon, the whole technique of fishing and trapping—in trapping the animal's strength and instinct was exploited, used against the animal (the idea must have originated from a time when man still felt himself completely inferior to the animal); then there was the use of poisons, and finally the attempt to gain spiritual power over the animal or the whole environment.

The hunter saw in the picture of an animal its soul-force, its spiritual being, and believed that by painting pictures he could capture and influence its soul-force.

Among the Australian aborigines—who remain today at the level of the early Stone Age hunters—rock-paintings depicting animals and plants are, every year, not repainted but touched up, so that new, powerful 'souls' may go out from them and take on new bodies.

Thus early man, the hunter, believed that in a spiritual manner, through art, he could intervene in the productive processes of nature and influence them in a way favourable to himself.

The figure of the shaman grows out of the world-picture of the hunter as a logical consequence. The development of the shaman as the prototype of the thinking of a

1   *Clay sculpture of the Magdalenian period. France*

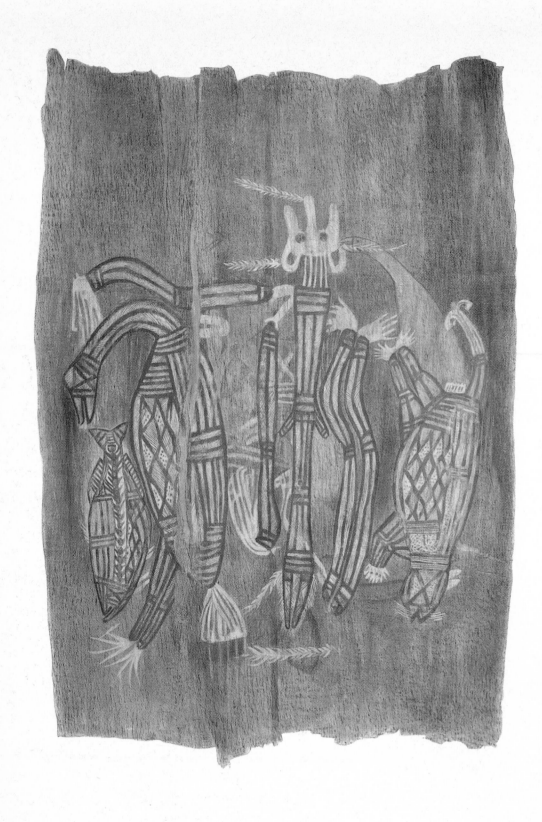

2 *Bark-painting from Australia*
3 *Right: the shaman Tulayev of the Karagass. Siberia*

4   *The Eskimo shaman Najagneq*

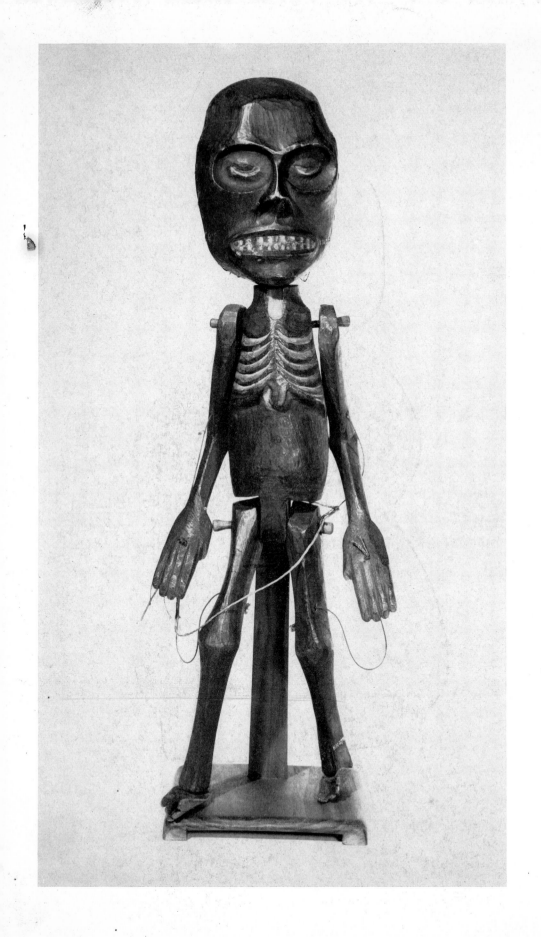

5 *Doll from north-west America*

6, 7 *Figure of a bear with a small human figure. North-west America*

8   *Small wooden figure of a singing shaman. North-west America*

hunting community can be seen on the one hand from the illuminating reports of the primitives, for example the Eskimos or the Siberians, which it was still possible to record at the beginning of the century; while, on the other, there are a wealth of observations made by European investigators in all parts of the world which, when put together, provide a general view of the various, but fundamentally similar, conceptions of the nature of the shaman.

Rock-engraving from North Africa

From these reports we can without difficulty describe the psychological phenomenon of shamanism, we can clearly grasp the inner development and psychic evolution of the shaman, but we are left uncertain as to the technique and the extent of its effect. True, the importance of the shaman for the community, the group, is clear, but the manner in which he operates is difficult to understand.

An important part of the shaman's effectiveness lies in his artistic productivity. Curiously enough, right up to the present day, this has been largely overlooked. And yet there are a great number of reports in which the shamans' artistic activity, above all their dramatic gifts, their use of theatrical effects, are clearly stated. That the shamans are magnificent poets and word-creators is sufficiently proved by the sagas which tell of their deeds and their technique, often composed by themselves.

But also visual art, and above all the rock-paintings, are partially derived from shamanism, as is shown by a study of certain motifs and a comparison between artistic motifs and mythological ideas.

It becomes clear that the shaman must be distinguished and differentiated from the ordinary medicine man as someone special, someone on a higher plane by virtue of his intellectual intensity—a figure who at a very early period crystallized out of the world and ideas of the early hunting community, and wherever he still emerges in a tangible shape, or could still be investigated a few decades ago, represents the form and nature of, if not the first, then at least a very early phase in human thinking.

This early thinking is expressed in the shaman's function as priest and doctor—though we must avoid drawing firm conclusions on this point from the present-day representatives of these functions.

The shaman is undoubtedly, perhaps essentially, a doctor—but the factual medical knowledge of the primitives is very small; the shaman's medical function seems to be confined to psychological, perhaps psychoanalytical techniques, and his successes fall mainly within the psychological domain.

Here our interest is aroused, for we see that the shaman—all reports point to this—is superior as a psychologist, a psychotherapist, to his modern colleagues, and in relation to psychosomatic disorders is able to advance much farther into the psychological aspect than a modern doctor. His technique seems to be far in advance of that of the modern psychotherapist. The shaman works only in a state of trance. He puts himself in a trance by means of monotonous sounds—drumming and the like, or dancing, or both—and this trance is then transmitted to his audience. The audience do not remain onlookers, but become participants. The state of trance is, so to speak, the plane of communication on which the healing psychological effect takes place. This goes far beyond the widespread and usual technique of the medicine man, who uses suggestion on his patients without going into a trance.

Shamans in bison masks with reindeer

Ostrich in magic circle. Rock-engraving from North Africa

Certain psychological experiences seem to be a prerequisite for the development of the shaman and the successful exercise of his functions. There can be no doubt as to the shaman's success as the regulator of the collective soul; this is proved by all reports. Naturally this is not due solely to him, but also to his patients. Primitive man is psychologically highly unstable and probably much more susceptible to influence than modern man is—or was, since his susceptibility to influence seems to be increasing with his growing dependence on the so-called mass media. The epoch of the independent, rational, and rationalist man who thinks for himself, as created and moulded by the European Enlightenment and the French Revolution, is drawing rapidly to a close. The modern mass-man is much closer to the primitive group-man than the solitary individual was a few decades ago.

The development of shamanism from the ideas of the hunting community

The basis of the intellectual outlook or conception of the world of hunters is the view that a living creature, every living creature, is divided into a physical and a spiritual being. A complex of spiritual or psychic substances is present, separable from the body, but apparently linked to particular parts of the body, such as bones, skin, horns. From these particular parts of the body and the 'souls' linked to them a creature can be repeatedly brought back to life. This intellectual conception, which then becomes a religious one and invents the concept of the 'immortal soul', leads in the thinking of the early hunters to tentative attempts to understand, explain, and also to master the world as spiritual life. From this conception there arises art: the picture of an animal contains its soul substance; through the picture a species of animal can be kept alive or brought back to life. This conception may explain the origin of early hunters' art, but it certainly does not explain the high artistic quality of the early rock-paintings nor the steady decline of this quality down to the primitive scribbles of the still living Eskimos or the Australians who still paint on the rocks.

Within the framework of this conception of the world there sprang up a particular psychic technique. Attempts were made, in the form of the trance, to penetrate into the spiritual world and exercise an influence on it. In the trance the hunter sends out his 'soul' to operate in the spirit world. At the same time he takes into himself 'souls', so-called 'helping spirits', which assist him in his work. The shaman separates his soul from his body and afterwards lets it return, just as in the case of an animal which the hunter kills the soul is separated from the body and made to enter into a picture and then into another animal.

The efficacy of the shaman relates to good luck in hunting and the healing of illnesses. He always banishes evil spirits and calls in good spirits to aid him. It is in many instances clear that the helping spirits are the spirits of the ancestors, so that the psychic power of generations is accumulated in him.

Along with the art of rock-painting, it is the figure of the shaman that interests us most in the culture of the early hunters. The quality of this early artistic expression is inexplicable and will remain an enigma. The art of the early hunters makes a mockery of all art-historical theories regarding the evolution of art, and therefore it will always remain an object of research. In the shaman we have, as it were, a concentration of the spiritual essence of the hunting culture, a figure in which this early way of thinking reaches its acme and which still exists in various regions of the earth, above all in northern Asia, North America, and in certain parts of Africa, down to our own time.

How did this figure come into being?

God of the ocean, Anky-Kele. Drawing from the Chukchee

Anisimov seeks, on the basis of his investigations in Siberia, to demonstrate the transformation from general hunting magic to the particular forms of shamanism. He indicates that the hunters' efforts to animate and dominate nature through the magic of spiritual forces evolves towards two culminating points, two poles. One is the concentration of the spiritual forces in the so-called Lord of the Animals, the other the genesis of the shaman as the representative of the magic powers which the hunters and their community seek to exercise.

The ideas connected with the word Shingken, the designation of the Lord of the Animals among various Tungus tribes, vary. At one time the Lord of the Animals may be in the sky, on the 'third cloud', or he may be everywhere in surrounding nature, in rocks, rivers, and in the taiga, or at the foot of bushes.

The whole of nature, including the animals, belongs to the Lord of the Animals; the welfare of men depends upon him. He disposes of his property, he can at will give it away or barter it, or else gamble or drink it away. But since he is very niggardly, he gives it to men only when he receives offerings from them.

The Lord of the Animals has a materially conceived assistant: an idol carved from wood representing either a small human figure without arms or a zoomorphic figure, mostly an elk. If the little idol is portrayed as a human figure it is dressed in a deerskin cap and a skirt of bear's ear skin.

Before the hunt the hunter appeals to the idol, not directly to the Lord of the Animals; he feeds the idol by throwing pieces of fat into the fire; he amuses it by dancing in front of it; finally he throws the idol into the air. If it falls with its face uppermost, this is a good omen for hunting or fishing; if it falls with its face downwards, this is a sign that the hunt will be unsuccessful.

The hunter sets conditions for the idol.

If the hunt is successful, he will give it new clothes; if it is not successful, he threatens to beat it. The Tungus say that in the past hunters prayed direct to Shingken and to rocks, lakes or the taiga as a whole to send good hunting, with the words:

> *Great father, great mother, mountains, rivers,*
> *hear us, have mercy, open the doors,*
> *that the spirits of the sables may come out.*

Later this request was transferred to the idol.

The idol is reinforced with numerous amulets. It is hung with little horses, tufts of hair, animals' teeth, the lower jaws of the elk and other animals. Often the space occupied by all these attached amulets is far greater than that occupied by the idol itself.

The idols are kept in a 'holy bag' and carried during migrations by a specially holy reindeer. The idols play an important role and are generally confused with the spirit whose helper they are and are themselves called Shingken.

An especially good hunter is said to possess an exceptionally diligent and benevolent idol.

The cult and worship of Shingken is taken over by the shaman. The shaman goes to the spirit Shingken and asks him to give men animals. This journey to the spirit begins with drumbeats. The shaman then falls to the ground, no doubt in a trance; it is then assumed that the Lord of the Animals has entered into him; he is laid on his back on a carpet and the audience wait until he wakes again. Then at the order of the shaman an anthropomorphic idol is constructed, through whose parted legs all the hunters have to crawl carrying their weapons. This act is called *Shingken lavun*, the catching of Shingken.

In earlier times the whole tribe took part in such ritual acts. The shaman went first to a sacred stone beneath which the spirit of Mother Earth lived. He asked her for help. She then sent him to the spirit of the Mother of the Whole World. This deity was represented as an outsize elk cow. From her he received permission to 'catch' animals. The shaman then led the animals he had caught into the hunting area of the tribe. On his return home he recounted how many animals he had caught. If it seemed too few, he had to repeat the journey (this journey was, of course, a dream journey under-taken in a state of trance).

The spirit of Mother Earth has on her breast a leather bag in which are preserved hairs and pieces of fur of all the animals—that is to say, parts of animals. The shaman asks the spirit woman to be allowed to look for lice on her. She allows him to do so, and in this way he steals hairs and pieces of fur. On his way home he scatters these all over the taiga. The pieces of animal then turn into real animals. The tribe's delight in a successful journey of this kind is expressed in a pantomimic dance. A kind of stage is erected, leaves are collected to represent the taiga, birds and animals carved of wood are placed on small branches. The hunt is portrayed and afterwards repeated in this theatri-cal form.[5]

Helping spirits which accompany the shaman on his journey to the Kingdom of the Dead. Goldi, Siberia

Ruler of the Whales. Painted wooden pendant from the Alaska Eskimos

Among the Eskimos there are historical accounts,[6] which Rasmussen has collected, concerning the genesis of the shaman out of the ideas of the hunting community as well as others of a more psychological nature testifying to the development of the shaman as a particular, positively ineluctable evolution of the individual.

These basic views remain extraordinarily alike among the hunters of North Africa, through Siberia to Alaska. Starting from a very weak position, man has to try to assert himself in his environment and, after imagining that he has discovered that nature may be divided into 'physical' and 'spiritual' entities or forces, to try to gain power over things, beings, his environment and above all over animals, on the spiritual plane. Dealing with the 'souls' of animals is dangerous and requires special ability and experience. Knowledge, wisdom, and power over souls are the most important things for man. Naturally it is exceptionally difficult for us to grasp the ideas linked with these words and concepts in the minds of the hunters. The spiritual world, represented by 'spirits', is a world of traditional notions—images, shaped by tradition, which these people carry in their minds, with which they play and work, and which they act out in the continual, lifelong struggle with the spirits.

Old Eskimos whom Rasmussen questioned gave detailed accounts of these notions:

All true wisdom is only to be found far from men, out in the great solitude, and it can only be acquired by suffering. Privations and sufferings are the only things that can open a man's mind to that which is hidden from others.

A man does not become a raiser of spirits because he wishes it himself, but because certain mystic powers outside in the universe give him to understand that he is chosen; this takes place through a revelation in dreams.

This mystic power, which so strongly affects men's destinies, is called *sila* and is very hard to define. The word has three meanings: universe, weather (good or bad) and a mixture of common sense, understanding and intelligence. In its religious sense the word *sila* is used for a power that can be taken possession of by men, a power that is personified in Sila Inua, the Lord of Power or, literally, 'he who possesses power'. The term *pinga* is often used, a spirit in the form of a woman who resides somewhere in the universe and appears only when she is needed. There is no clear idea that she is the

Rock-engraving from North Africa, so-called *en-face* lion. This drawing was of great importance for the hunting magic of the early hunters in North Africa

Rock-engraving at Tiout, North Africa. Magical scene, perhaps a Mistress of the Animals or hunting goddess who helps the hunter

creator of the world or that the beasts of the chase are descended from her, but everyone fears her as a strict housekeeper who watches over all men's actions, particularly the way in which they treat the animals they hunt.

Furthermore, all taboos are directed towards Sila and are intended to maintain the balance of men's relationship to this power. The conditions which Sila imposes upon men are not strict, but perhaps for that very reason he uses his power to punish all infringements; he punishes by causing bad weather or by driving the animals from the tribe's hunting-grounds with sickness—in fact, the punishment consists in the misfortune that is most feared. Thus the reindeer Eskimos live in constant conflict with Sila and with themselves. In this conception we can catch a glimpse of a conscious wisdom which deserves every respect.

A shaman is the intermediary between Sila and men. His main function is to heal sick people or free them from other evils. If a sick man is to be saved, he must give away all possessions. These have to be carried away and laid on the ground far from the dwellings; for when a man calls upon a great spirit he must not possess anything but his own breath.[7] It is said that in olden times, when the sea creatures came into being, there were not yet any reindeer on land. But an old woman wandered into the land and created them. She made their skin out of her own trousers, so that the distribution of the hair varied in the same way as the pattern on her trousers. But the reindeer received teeth like other animals. And originally it even had tusks. It was a dangerous animal, and it was not long before a man was killed while hunting. Then the old woman was afraid; she went into the land again and gathered together the reindeer she had created. She turned the tusks into horns, she knocked out the front teeth, and when she had done this she said to them: 'Land animals like you should stay far from men and be timid!' Then she gave them a kick on the forehead, which is the cause of the dent that can be seen on the forehead of all reindeer. The reindeer galloped away and after that were very shy.

But they soon proved to be too fast. No man could hunt them, and again the old woman had to catch them. This time she altered the arrangement of their hair, so that not all the hairs lay in the same direction. Now the hair on the shoulder, the hair under the throat and under the flanks ran in different directions. Then the animals were released again. Although the reindeer was still swift it no longer cut the air so easily, and men could catch up with it and kill it. Later the old woman settled among the reindeer and she is now called the Mother of the Reindeer.

In this way both the sea creatures and the reindeer received their mother and therefore they must never be dealt with at the same time. There is also another reason for exercising great prudence. All living creatures possess powers which make them particularly sensitive to the rules of life that have been assumed by men. These powers reside in the souls and in the names.

The soul or *inusia* is that which gives each living thing the particular appearance which it has. In fact, it is in man a very small man, in the reindeer a tiny reindeer and thus in all animals a miniature image of the carrier, and it sits in an air-filled bladder in the groin. From it comes the appearance, come thoughts, strength and life. It makes the man a man, the reindeer a reindeer, the walrus a walrus, the dog a dog and so on.

If violence is done to this soul or if it is injured by the infringement of a taboo, it becomes an evil spirit that brings misfortune and death. Aua puts it like this:

The greatest danger in life lies in the fact that man's food is made up of souls.

This means that special care must be taken of every animal that is slain or used for clothing and food, for every animal has a soul.[8]

Men have always been afraid of illness, and from the very earliest times men arose who tried to get to the bottom of all the incomprehensible things that surround mankind. At this time there were no raisers of spirits and men were ignorant of all the rules of life which they later learned to observe out of fear of danger and malignity. The first amulet was the shell of a sea-urchin. There is a hole through this, for which reason it bears the name *iteg* (anus), and it became the first amulet because a special healing power was ascribed to it. When a man fell ill another sat down beside him and passed wind while pointing at the sick part. Then this man went out while another held his hollowed hand over the sick spot, at the same time blowing his breath over the palm of the other hand. In this way, they thought, the wind and the breath combined all the force that comes out of the inside of a man, a force so mysterious and strong that it can heal.

Drawing of a spirit by an Eskimo artist

In this way all men were doctors, and therefore shamans were not necessary. But one day want and bad hunting descended upon the district round Igdlulik. Many died of hunger and there was great perplexity. Then it happened one day that many people were gathered in a house and a man, for no apparent reason, asked to be taken behind the skin curtain of the sleeping-bench. He said that he was going to go down to the Mother of the Sea Creatures. No one in the house understood him and no one believed him. They did as he asked and took him behind the skin curtain. There he said he wanted to practise an art which would henceforth be of great benefit to men. But no one must see him. But it was not long before the incredulous and curious raised the curtain; to their astonishment they discovered that he was in the act of diving down into the earth. He had already gone down so far that only the soles of his feet were visible. How the man had come upon this idea no one could say. He himself asserted that he was helped by spirits with whom he had made a pact out in the great solitude. Thus the first sorcerer came into being. He went down to the Mother of the Sea Creatures and brought back animals to be hunted, and the period of want was followed by good hunting and men were once more happy and joyful. Since then the shamans have developed their knowledge of the hidden things and help men in many ways. They also received their sacred language that is only used during the conjuring up of spirits and not in everyday speech.[9]

The numerous accounts of the psychological development of the shaman, many of them of impressive artistic quality and all of them very similar throughout the world, make it perfectly possible for us to reach certain conclusions regarding the nature of the shaman and to distinguish this figure from so-called magicians and medicine men.

Early man is helpless in the face of the 'hidden things'; the background of his world, its causes and effects, are mysterious and closed to him. In trying to understand the interconnexions he starts from the assumption that all things have souls, that there exists a spiritual force whose effects he believes he can feel everywhere. And there develop men, or a particular type of man, who devote themselves first to fathoming these interconnexions and then to mastering this soul-force.

The characteristic features of this type of man are again described by the Eskimos, as well as the psychological preconditions which is demanded. These descriptions refer to certain laws of behaviour, which are believed to have been established as valid after long experience, the so-called 'taboos', a term that has been taken over into anthropology from the Polynesian world.

Infringements of taboo bring misfortune, sickness, and death upon men, and it seems that an unfortunate, sick man has a greater ability to rectify such infringements of the law than an ordinary healthy man. In any case, there are frequent references to the fact that the shaman must have overcome inhibitions and illnesses, that he was or is a sick man, a man in every way 'underprivileged', a man who began his life with a false start. The shaman is a man of complex psychological make-up who must arouse the interest of the modern psychologist all the more because here the surprising intricacy and complexity of the 'primitive psyche' once more becomes visible.

Drawing of a spirit by an Eskimo artist. The sorceress Manilaq (Cake-Ice). The artist met her in the summer while roaming in the mountains. She looked so terrifying that he fell down and lost consciousness and only recovered when the dog licked his navel. She became his helping spirit

The development of the shaman—accounts from the Eskimos

Apart from the great importance which the shaman had in his priestly or medical function among almost all northern peoples, from the Lapps through the peoples of the whole of Siberia, Alaska, and Canada to Greenland (and to some extent still has), he is in the first place an extraordinarily interesting and as yet totally unexplained phenomenon of self-healing.

There are accounts derived from the Eskimos according to which people who, because of an originally sickly and frail constitution, appear ill equipped for the struggle for existence, seem predestined to become shamans and are laboriously kept alive by those around them through the observation of all possible safety precautions and 'taboo regulations', and made into shamans.

Thus Rasmussen tells the story of an Eskimo shaman:

'I was still no more than a small fruit in my mother's body when people began to enquire after me sympathetically. All the children which my mother had borne up to now had lain crosswise and had been born dead. As soon as my mother noticed that she was carrying a child that was to become myself she spoke like this to the other people in the house: "Now I am once more carrying a fruit that will not become a human being!" Everyone was very sorry for her, and a woman named Artjuaq, who was a shamaness, that same evening performed a conjuration of spirits in order to help my mother. The very next day people could see that I had grown, but this did me no good at the time, because the shamaness had forgotten that on the day after the conjuration she was not allowed to do any work. But she had sewed up a hole in a mitten. This breaking of a taboo immediately affected me. My mother began her labour pains too soon, and I wriggled and worked as though trying to get out through her side. A fresh conjuration was held, and as this time all the taboos were rigorously observed it helped both my mother and me. But then one day it happened that my father, who was about to set out on a hunting trip, was angry and agitated; to calm him, my mother started helping him to harness the sledge. She forgot that in her condition all work was taboo for her. No sooner had she taken a dog harness and lifted the paw of one of the dogs to harness it, than I immediately began to kick and tried to get out through her navel, and again a raiser of spirits had to come to our aid.

'Everyone now told my mother that my great sensitivity to all infringements of taboo was a sign that I should live and become a great shaman. But at the same time much danger and discomfort would pursue me until I was born.

'My father had caught a walrus that was pregnant; when he tried to cut out the fruit, without thinking that my mother was with child, I once again began to wriggle in the womb, and this time it was serious. But at the same moment in which I was born, all life left me, and I lay stone-dead. My mother's after-birth had wrapped itself round my throat and strangled me. Artjuaq, who lived in another village, was fetched at once and a special lying-in house was built for my mother. When the shamaness came and saw that my eyes were popping out of my head, she dried my mother's blood from my body with a raven's skin and sewed a little jacket for me of the same material.

' "He is born to die, but he will live," she said. And then Artjuaq stayed with my mother until life came back into me. My mother had to undergo a special diet and difficult taboo rules. For example, if she had eaten of a walrus, this walrus became taboo to everyone else. It was the same with seals and reindeer. She had to have her own pots, from which no one else was allowed to eat; no woman was allowed to visit her, but men were allowed to. My clothes were sewn in a particular way. The hairs of the skin must never run upwards or downwards, but always at right-angles to my body. Thus I lived in the lying-in house with no inkling of all the care that was being taken of me.

'For a whole year my mother and I had to live alone and were only rarely allowed visits from my father. Although as a great hunter he was always out hunting, he was never allowed to sharpen his own knife; as soon as he did so, his hand swelled and I fell ill. A year after my birth we were allowed to take a woman house-companion; but whenever she was compelled to go out she had to take the precaution of putting her hood over her head, wearing boots without stockings and holding up the hem of her fur with one hand.

'I was already a big boy before my mother was allowed, for the first time, to go visiting. Everyone was kind to her and she was invited to all the inhabitants of our village. But she stayed away too long. The spirits do not like to see women with small children staying away from home too long, and they took revenge by making the skin on her head peel. I myself, who at that time understood nothing about all this, struck her body with my little hands, and as we were going home I passed water down her back.

'No one who wants to be a skilful hunter or a good shaman must stay too long on a visit to a strange house. The same applies to a woman so long as she is carrying a boy in her back-bag.

'Finally I became so big that I was allowed to go hunting for seals by the breathing-holes with the adults. On the day on which I harpooned my first seal, my father had to lie on the ice with a naked torso, and the seal which I had caught was dragged over his back for as long as there was life in it. Only men were allowed to eat of my first catch

Drawing of a shaman's tent. From the Evenks, Siberia

and nothing was allowed to be left over. The skin and the head were hidden out on the ice, so that later I could catch the same seal again. For three days and three nights none of the men who had taken part in the meal were allowed to go hunting or to do any other work.

'My next quarry was a reindeer. It was strictly forbidden for me to use a gun; I had to kill it with bow and arrow. This animal too was eaten by men only, no woman was allowed to touch it. Then some time passed and I became grown-up and strong enough to go walrus hunting. When I harpooned my first walrus, my father shouted as loudly as he could, giving the names of all the inhabitants of the village known to him and crying: "Now there is meat for everyone!"

'The walrus was dragged ashore while there was still life in it and not killed completely until it was on the beach. My father, who was to cut up the blubber, was tied to the cord before the point of the harpoon was removed from the animal's body. After I had slain this walrus I was allowed to eat all those titbits that had previously been forbidden to me, even the entrails, and now the women were also allowed to eat of my catch, as long as they were not women in childbed. Only my mother still had to be careful for a very long time, and whenever she had to sew, a special house was built for her. I was named after a minor spirit called Aua, and people said my mother must observe all sorts of precautions in order not to offend him; he was my guardian spirit and watched very closely to see that nobody did anything forbidden. Thus I was never allowed to stay in an igloo in which young women were undressing to go to bed. Nor was my wife allowed to do her hair in my presence. For a long time after my marriage there was still a strict taboo on animals I had killed. When there were women in childbed living near us, my wife was only allowed to eat animals killed by me. But on walruses which I had killed there was a taboo that no woman was allowed to eat of their entrails, and this taboo was maintained until I was the father of four children. And really it is only now, when I am old, that those obligations have been abolished which were established by the old shamaness that I might live.

'Most feared of all the helping spirits was the ermine of the sea. This was shaped just like the ermine of the land, only more slender, more supple and swifter, and it could shoot up out of the sea so suddenly that it was impossible to defend oneself. It had black shiny skin and no hair, apart from a little at the tip of the tail and on the lobes of the ears.

'When a man was out with a kayak, it often used to leap up like lightning from the depths and slip into his sleeves; as it ran about over his naked body it filled him with such horror that he almost lost consciousness.

'It was the task of the trained sorcerer to heal the sick, to go down to the Land of the Dead and look for lost souls, to go down to the Mother of the Sea to fetch animals to be hunted, to perform miraculous feats that amazed men and convinced them of the shaman's astounding abilities.

'The cause of almost all illnesses was the stealing of souls. This might be the work of hostile shamans or of people who dealt in magic. Such people were easily angered and derived from their evil excitement the power to squeeze the soul out of the body. If the soul was not brought back, the sick man was bound to die. The sicknesses of little children usually came from the breaking of taboos by the mother, and it was the shaman's task to find out where the offence lay.

'Now that I have become a Christian, I have sent my helping spirits down to my sister in Baffin Land. But if you want to know more about shamans I will tell you about my cousin Niviatsian, whom the spirits called to themselves in a fantastic manner that he might become a great shaman.'[10]

Another account given by Rasmussen goes as follows:

'Niviatsian was hunting walrus with many other men near Igdlulik. Suddenly a great walrus came up out of the ice right beside him, seized him with its mighty front flippers, as a mother takes hold of her little child, and carried him down into the depths. The other men hurried to the spot, and as they looked down into the hole in the ice through which the walrus had vanished, they could see that it was holding him tightly squeezed in its embrace and was trying to bore through him with its tusks. After a while it let go of him and came to the surface far, far away to get air. But Niviatsian, who had moved away from the hole through which he had been pulled down, was now working with his arms and legs to get to the surface again. The men could follow his movements and made a hole just about where they expected him to come up, and here my father was actually able to pull him out. He had a gaping wound by the collarbone, through which he was breathing. The gash went down into the lung. Some of the ribs were broken and the broken ends had penetrated one lung, so that he could not stand up straight.

'Niviatsian lay for a long time unconscious. When he came to himself again, he was able to rise without help. The wound by the collarbone was the only serious injury. Traces of the walrus's tusks could be seen on his head as well as round his body, but it was as though the walrus had been unable to injure him. Old people said that this walrus had been sent by the Mother of the Sea Creatures, because she was angry with Niviatsian's wife for having concealed an abortion in order not to have to submit to the taboo. Niviatsian then followed his comrades ashore, but he had to walk a little way away from them on the ice where there were no footprints. On land nearby a small igloo was built and here he was shut up and placed on a small scrap of seal skin, with all his wet clothes on his body. Here he sat for three days and three nights without food and drink. He had to do this in order to be allowed to live, for if he had at once gone to the impure dwellings of men, he would inevitably have died after the maltreatment he had suffered.

'During the whole time that Niviatsian was sitting in the little igloo, the sorcerer in the village was continuously busy purifying his wife and his old mother, who had to confess their infringement of the taboo in the presence of everyone, in order to pacify the powers that control life and death. Niviatsian recovered in three days and was then a great shaman. The walrus that had not been able to kill him became his first helping spirit. That was the beginning.

'Another time, when he was hunting reindeer, he ran straight into the den of a wolverine. The wolverine had young and therefore attacked him furiously. It wrestled with him all day and all night and did not let him go until the sun was at the same point again as when they began. In spite of its sharp claws and teeth, the wolverine had not been able to bite a single hole in his body and had only scraped off a little of his skin. Thus the wolverine became his helping spirit.

'His third helping spirit was Amajorjuk, a giantess with an enormous carrying-bag on her back into which she put the people whom she carried off. She fell upon him so suddenly that he found himself already in her bag before he could do anything to defend himself. The neck of the bag immediately closed over him and he was shut in. But he had his knife hanging round his neck and with this he stabbed the giantess in the back just behind the shoulder-blade, so that she fell dead. The carrying-bag was as thick as walrus hide and it took him a long time to cut his way out and get free. But then he discovered that he was completely naked. He had no idea when he had taken off his clothes, nor where, only that it must have been far, far inland. He did not find his clothes until he was approaching the sea, and he returned home unharmed. But he had a horrible stench of rotting seaweed all over his body, and this stench continued in his house. It went on for half a year, when it disappeared again. This giant woman also became his helping spirit, and after that he was looked upon as the greatest shaman among men.

'So—according to Aua—there were two ways of becoming a conjurer-up of spirits: either a man went out to seek the spirits in solitude, or they came to him of their own accord, in a mysterious and violent fashion, and it was precisely the sudden fear that opened his eyes.'[11]

Drawing of a spirit by an Eskimo artist. Igtuk or the Thunderer. When thunder rumbles in the mountains he is the cause of the noise.

The development of the shaman—accounts from Siberia

The word 'shaman' comes from the Tungus language. Comparisons with similar words in Mongolian and Manchurian indicate that all these words designate a certain excited, restless state.

The shaman is frequently a person of unstable constitution and restless, at times abstracted, behaviour. He is an eccentric who frequently withdraws from the community to devote himself wholly to his visions and dreams.

A call to shamanhood is first manifested either in the gradual appearance of seizures, which may either be convulsive or else show hysteroid or epileptoid features, so that in the case of certain peoples they are referred to as 'arctic hysteria'; or a call comes to the future shaman in the form of 'chance occurrences'.

Thus Nioradze reports that the novices in Siberia display a shy nature, avoid human company and flee into the forests, there to listen in seclusion for their inner voice.

In some accounts these abnormal states are described as spasmodic seizures which, especially in youth, but occasionally also at an advanced age, come over the future shaman, so that he completely loses consciousness and no longer knows where he is. In violent seizures he yells and rages like a madman, destroying everything that comes in his way. There are also reports of a cataleptic state known in the Russian literature as hysterical rigidity or the 'bridge'. 'The future shamans had violent seizures that ended in total exhaustion. They lay motionless for two or three days, without eating or drinking. Finally they ran into the forests and there went hungry.'[12]

Particularly after events which make high demands upon his emotional life, such as visions and ghostly apparitions, the future shaman frequently has seizures which are accompanied by a rigidity that renders his body stiff and devoid of feeling. 'After a dream apparition the dreamer became very ill, went into a trance, and his body was as stiff as a board.'[13]

Czaplicka also states that future shamans have violent seizures which end in total exhaustion, so that they lie motionless for two or three days without food.[14]

Prior to this, wild frenzy may occur that is turned against objects and the sufferer's own person. 'The future shaman behaves like a madman, sometimes quite benumbed by his fits, and then again fearful.' 'During the fits they have a tendency to injure themselves, either to jump into the water or to run into fire.'[15]

In an attack such as this, which is linked with disturbances of consciousness, the sufferers run out of their houses and remain for days in the forest—they are found hiding in caves or up in trees and can be brought home only by force. 'Crimes and sudden acts of brutality are not infrequent among these people.'[16]

Alongside pure convulsive states there are also epileptoid and hysteroid states which, as in disorders of this kind known in Europe, are connected with partial convulsions.

Radloff relates in his journal *Out of Siberia*: 'The power of shamanhood comes upon the individual like a sickness falling upon him. The individual who is destined to become a shaman feels a lassitude in his limbs that proclaims itself through a violent trembling. Violent, unnatural yawning comes over him; an enormous pressure rests upon his chest; he feels a sudden urge to utter violent and inarticulate cries; he is shaken by a shivering fit; he rolls his eyes, suddenly jumps up and runs round in a circle as though possessed, until he falls, bathed in sweat, and twists about on the ground in epileptic twitching and spasms.'[17] The appearance of these symptoms described as 'epileptic' (other investigators actually speak in this connexion of 'frothing at the mouth') is not, however, in our opinion a sufficient criterion for the presence of real epilepsy; what we see here is probably a constitution which in its outward manifestation seems to correspond to that termed by Kraepelin hysterical.

According to Kraepelin, the extreme form of hysteria is characterized by 'fainting fits, confused excitement, lashing out in all directions, rearing up, grinding the teeth, trembling and attacks of cramp. The sufferers sink to the ground, display a rigidity of the eyelids and after waking stretch and twist their limbs, shiver, wriggle, roll over, bite and shout.'[18] In view of the similarity of Radloff's account there seems to be a certain justification in speaking of hysterical disposition in the shaman, as some observers do, for example Schirokogorow: 'We see hysterical seizures with all the typical concomitants, cramps, the bridge, fear of the light, etc.'[19] Phenomena such as those described by Charcot as *grande hysterie* may also be mentioned in this connexion. The symptom of the 'hysterical bridge and rigidity' corresponds to Charcot's *arc de cercle*. In this condition the hysteric lies on the backs of two chairs, his head on one and his heels on the other. He is in a cataleptic condition, that is to say so stiff that in many cases he can bear an additional heavy weight.[20] Thus the condition described by Schirokogorow is probably a phenomenon related to hysteria. Troshansky also attributes the disposition of the shaman to a phenomenon that is similar to hysteria—*memerik*, meaning the spirit of ecstasy.

Schirokogorow likewise describes 'the hysterical fit of a shamaness who was possessed by a pregnant spirit and developed a swollen abdomen, so that people thought she was going to give birth on the spot'.[21] This symptom points to a hysteroid disposition similar to the well-known cases of hysterical pregnancy.

With reference to other peoples the expression 'arctic hysteria' is frequently employed in ethnological literature. This type of hysteria is termed arctic because it occurs chiefly within the arctic zone.[22] Following Jochelson and Prikonsky, a distinction is made between two different forms of arctic hysteria:

Amürakh is a malady in which the sufferer is easily frightened and has a tendency to imitate everything he sees taking place around him. He shows a special proclivity for indulging in obscenities.[23]

Prikonsky describes the same nervous disorder among the Yakut as follows:

'The attack of *amürakh* is generally manifested in a groundless, instantaneous imitation of another person. A sudden shout uttered by another person is enough to make the sufferer shudder with terror and repeat his model's every movement, no matter how wanton.'[24]

The second form of arctic hysteria is the *memerik* already referred to, which is of particular interest to us here in judging the predisposition to shamanhood. In the language of the Tungus this word means something like mad or possessed by an evil spirit. The disease chiefly attacks those aspirants to shamanhood who are still young. Its symptoms have been described as follows:

The disorder proper is unleashed by fright. From the moment this fright is suffered, the disorder periodically recurs. It reaches its acme in the trance, when the sufferer 'howls and dances'; finally the process ends with 'epileptic seizures'.

The *memerik* state is considered a sort of certificate of suitability for the future shaman. 'A youth who has suffered from *memerik* has the better chance of becoming a shaman. In all cases this illness is ascribed to evil spirits, but for the shaman it is a desirable struggle with evil and an exercise in which he learns how to appease these spirits, while an ordinary mortal is only a victim of *kelet* or *abassy*, a "sick person". . . . If a shaman cannot control or invoke the spirits at the right time, he ceases to be a shaman.'[25] It is important here that the future shaman must have overcome the sickness *memerik* in a way that marks him off from the ordinary person. We might say that in order to exercise his function as a healer of souls—one of his major tasks—the shaman must first have himself experienced his patients' sufferings. The attack by this ailment is to be understood as a kind of test which the would-be shaman has to undergo. For only that man who has successfully battled with the spirit world, that is to say with the forces within himself, can help his fellow tribesmen and assist them in his roles of priest, doctor, and prophet, that is to say as an intermediary with the 'spirit world'.

The call—by sickness, animals, dreams

There are some tribes in which the individual believes that he sees in some event, which may take place, for example, in connexion with his work, an indication that he is later to become a shaman. To him each of these signs, which would appear to us mere coincidences, has a meaning. Thus within the framework of this thinking the gushing forth of water when a tree is struck, for example, is taken to be a miraculous sign, a call to the office of shaman. This way of thinking corresponds to an affective, egocentric conception of the world; that is to say, chance events seem always to be grouped round the individual as their focal point and are arbitrarily interpreted by him. In this way purely chance signs and occurrences appear to be linked in a meaningful and ordered context. Of many similar examples we will quote here only one typical one. Gusinde gives an account of a young Tierra del Fuego Indian who was seeking a suitable piece of wood for his harpoon shaft.[26] When he found a tree and was about to fell it, to his astonishment water gushed out of it. 'He was seized with fright and recognized this sign. He hurried straight home to his hut, and without wasting another word he asked his wife and children not to touch him, speak to him or disturb him, but to keep quite quiet. He lay down and in no time was in a deep sleep.' The individual spirits appeared to him in a dream and talked to him in a friendly manner. One of the spirits offered himself as an assistant and told him that he must without fail become a shaman. This was his call.[27]

The development of a shaman, the psychological evolution from sickness through self-cure to the ability to shamanize, passes through many stages which are clearly described in the accounts—once again they appear in the form of metaphors, as outward events, whereas they are, of course, inner events.

Dreams are often referred to, and they, too, are also described as if they were the experience of an outer, 'real' world.

The period of preparation is frequently preceded by a mystic experience on the part of the shaman in which, so to speak, he gives up his personality in order to be born again into another individuality. The shaman's true preparation for his office is then carried out either by a real teacher or by one who appears to him in a dream.

During the period of preparation the shaman displays to a heightened degree those mental peculiarities already described, which manifest themselves particularly in visions, a need for solitude and prolonged swoons. This preparatory period, the 'first in-dwelling of the spirits', as it is called among the Tungus, is by no means a pleasant one for the young man. 'The Buryats believe that at such a time the boy's soul is with the spirits, who are teaching him. Dwelling in the palaces of the gods, the soul, under the guidance of the dead shamans, learns all the secrets of the shamanist craft; it remembers the names of the gods, their dwelling place, the forms used in their worship, and the names of the spirits subject to these great gods. After enduring trials, the soul returns to the body.'[28]

After this, the novice devotes himself whole-heartedly to executing the commands of his visions.

Even if the ethnographic literature always refers to dreams, less often to images and visions, we must nevertheless bear in mind that 'dreaming' is not an adequate expression for these phenomena that are unknown to us. Nevertheless, we shall continue to employ this designation for the sake of simplicity.

Often there appears to the aspirant a guiding authority who directs him and exercises the function of a teacher. From this authority he receives instructions as to his mode of life, for example concerning foods he is to avoid or prefer; he also learns from him which songs to practise, what words to say, what offerings to bring, what clothes to make and the like. In short, this dream authority furnishes him with the intellectual and practical equipment for his future office, in the process of which a certain similarity or actual overlapping with the 'called spirits' may often be observed.

In some instances the preparation is carried out by a human authority, for example an older shaman. The latter then has the special task of introducing his novice to shamanistic techniques and the spirit world.

Rasmussen gives excellent descriptions of the experiences of an aspirant shaman among the Canadian Eskimos.

'When a young man wished to become a shaman he had to make a gift of something from his property to the magician who was to be his teacher. Wood was regarded at Igdlulik as a particularly valuable commodity, and therefore it gradually came to be the custom to present a tent-pole. A gull's wing had to be attached to this tent-pole, as a sign that the apprentice wished to learn to fly through the air. The gift was set up outside the house as an offering to the helping spirits. In the evening the shaman had then to call upon his helping spirits to purify his apprentice's body and soul. In the presence of all he had to confess his infringements of taboo and his other misdemeanours. During the purification he had continually to cry out: "All this because I wish to become seeing!"

'The master had to remain behind a curtain placed in front of the sleeping-bench, the sacred place of sorcerers. When the apprentice was completely purified, he had to go behind the curtain. Here the shaman, concealed from all curious eyes, had to take out his apprentice's soul from his eyes, brain and entrails. This, it was said, filled the inside of the body with light, and a shaman had to be surrounded and pervaded by light.

'If the apprentice was a man, his brain, his eyes and his entrails could remain for three days without soul; if it was a woman, four days. During this time no work could be done in the house, and the pupil had to remain continually behind the curtain. It was believed that the power in his eyes, his brain and his entrails passed over during these days into his future helping spirits, so that he should have no fear of them if he one day saw them. And this could only happen far from men, out in the great solitude. For only in solitude could a man work his way closer to the spirits. But those who were to come to anything had to start very young, often indeed before they were born.'[29]

Among a Siberian tribe, the Goldi, a guardian spirit appears to the novice in a dream and takes over his guidance and training as a shaman. 'This guardian spirit teaches him

9 *'Ascent to Heaven' of a shaman. Thirteenth-century Chinese painting*

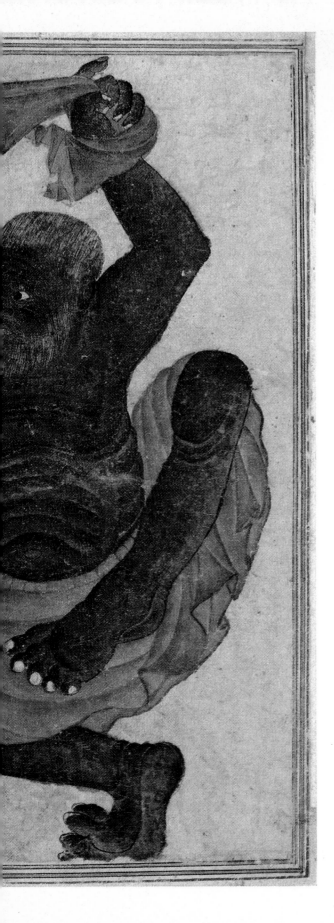

10 *Two wildly dancing shamans. Turkish, fifteenth century (see plates 11, 12, 13, and 15).*

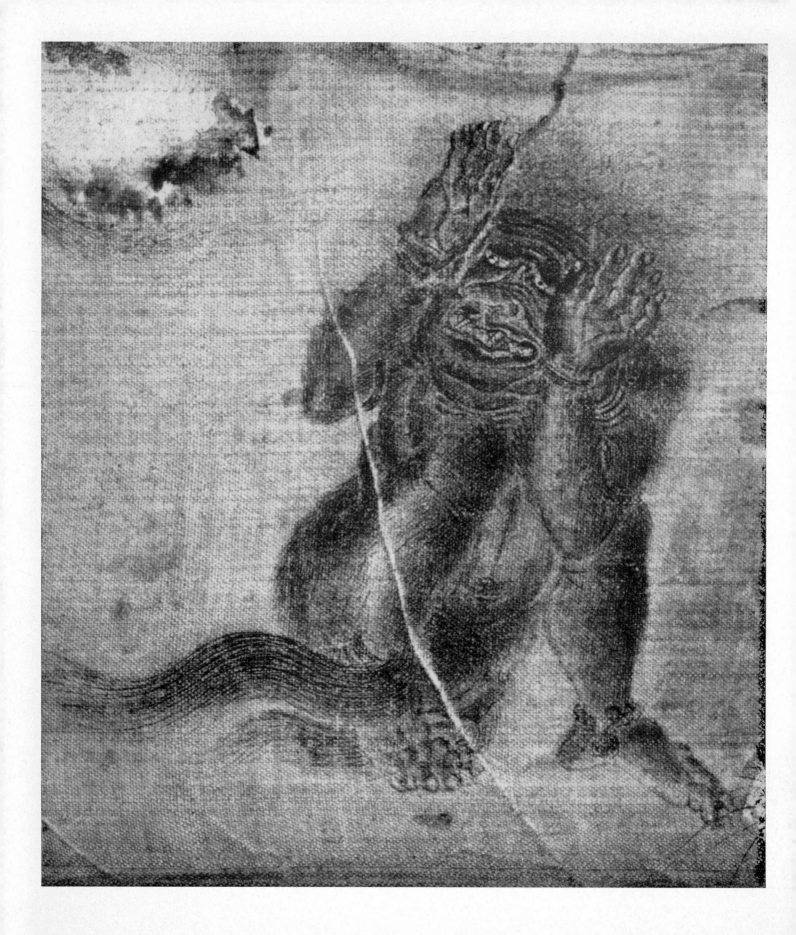

11 *Cowering demon (detail)*

12 *Spirits which have torn up the body of a horse and are fighting over the corpse*

13 *Two demons fighting*

everything he has to do, tells him what clothes he must wear and how they are to be made.'[30]

Further, he learns how to use the drum, how the spirits are to be stirred to activity and how he can separate his soul from his body in order to send it away.[31]

Further examples of preparation are to be met with among the Pima tribe of north-western America. The future shaman is visited in a dream by a teacher, perhaps in the shape of a little man, who teaches him songs and 'liturgical texts'. There then follows a seven-year training period, in which the shaman begins to practise his activity, first alone and then in the circle of his fellow tribesmen. If he is successful, his training is concluded by a further visit in a dream from the manikin, who this time tells him his name.

He then receives an outward symbol of his shamanist dignity, for instance a small splinter of glass, which he always has to carry with him. Now he is an approved shaman.[32]

The visionary powers of the aspirant shaman are developed to an even higher degree during the period of preparation among the Mohave of California. They receive instructions direct from Mastambo, who lived in the mythological epoch and is considered the founder of shamanism. Through his visions the dreamer is able to transport himself back into primeval times. During his dream experiences he is present at Mastambo's ceremonies and learns the songs from him. After this vision he is possessed of shamanistic powers.[33]

The call by an animal spirit is of particularly frequent occurrence in America, the more so as the sense of solidarity between man and animal is there so strong that the two are thought to be linked by a common ancestor. Thus it is often the animal ancestor who calls upon the novice to become a shaman. The relationship between man and animal is so close that the animal ancestor frequently appears in human form and is recognizable as an animal only by certain attributes.

Thus a Paviotso Indian reports having been called by an eagle in human shape: 'A tall, slender man stood in front of me. He said: "You want to be a shaman. You must do as I tell you. First get your eagle feathers and do what I tell you with them. You have chosen this and it may be hard for you. The feather is to guide you. You can bring the souls of dead people back with it. Do that, otherwise you will have a hard time. At the bottom of this cliff there is some water. Bathe in it and paint yourself with white paint. Don't be impatient but wait for my instructions." I did what he told me and I learned my songs and how to cure the sick when this tall man came to me in dreams.'[34]

Among the Tlingit Indians the man called to be a shaman dreams that an otter comes to him and he has to cut out its tongue. The call takes a similar form among the Penobscot Indians, where the shaman has to cut off the head of a snake that appears to him. This is a means of binding the snake spirit to him.

Other instances of calls by animals occur among the Californian Maricopa, who are called to the office of shaman by eagles, buzzards, coyotes, and horned owls.[35]

Another example of a call by an animal spirit is quoted by Gusinde from the Indians of Tierra del Fuego. 'The immediate call may come from true *cowanni* spirits. A man is wandering alone along the shore, as though lost in a dream world, without any particular mental images. Suddenly he finds himself translated into a state of spiritual horror known as *asikaku*: "before him crowds an endless swarm of herrings, whales, swordfish, vultures, cormorants, stormy petrels and other creatures. All of them talk to him flatteringly, prove amiable and utterly subservient to him and behave like the friendliest of human beings." That man is entirely out of his mind and does not know what is happening to him; his whole body insensible, he falls to the ground and lies motionless. His soul is associating with the *cowanni* spirits and experiences an extraordinary happiness in doing so. Suddenly the spirits take their leave and disappear. Awaking from the heavy dream, the man staggers home. He scarcely knows what is happening around him; he drops on to his bed and sinks back into his dream. Again the swarm of animals appears to him; all of them act with great friendliness towards him and entice his *kespix* (soul). Soon it (his soul) follows them far out on the high sea. One of the spirits then shows him an effusive kindliness; this will be the man's special guardian spirit; all the other spirits will also be at his disposal as friends and assistants. Those closest to the man recognize from his behaviour what is going on in him; they leave him unmolested and wait patiently until he has shaken off his heavy dream.'[36]

'If a man has a vision of a snake, all snakes will be fathers to him. Some were adopted by a bear. While they were asleep at home someone might strike the soul of a visionary's foot, then he would awake, make a noise like a bear, and a bear's tooth would come out of his mouth. This is one way of knowing the species of animal giving the vision. People who have seen a snake, do not kill snakes. Snake visionaries are mostly doctors; the snake tells them how to treat the sick.'[37]

In northwestern America and Australia we find frequent instances where the call was delivered by a snake. A Crow Indian gives an account of this. 'First we see a man in a vision or in a dream, but a few days later, when we are asleep, we realize that the human apparition was an animal that had turned itself into a man. Often the man who has been called notices this directly from the contents of the song. Thus the spirit may say in the song, for example: "I am a snake" (or a buffalo, or a horse etc).'[38]

When a man has a vision of a snake, this means that all snakes assume the status of fathers for him. After such a vision the visionary can, for example, pick up a snake and say to it, 'I am your son', and the snake will do him no harm.[39]

The Australian aborigines say that a man is made a shaman by certain experiences which descend upon him suddenly and unexpectedly.

Usually this 'experience of being called' is described as a dream, in which the soul of the future shaman does not journey to foreign countries, nor to the underworld of the dead, but into the deepest interior of the earth, where the creative power of the world—pictured as a snake—dwells in the depths of the water.

The aborigines say that various animals, especially snakes, assist the shaman on this journey and give him the strength, the 'medicine', for his office.

Such dreams of being called are described as follows: 'The soul of the man who is becoming a shaman leaves him. His body lies asleep. It is a deep sleep and no one dares to wake the sleeper, even if this sleep lasts for days. During the sleep the soul goes to the water-hole from which it originally came. It does not remain in this water-hole, however, but dives down from there into the innermost part of the earth. There, after a long

Drawing of a bear spirit. From Siberia

journey through dark water, it suddenly comes to a brightly lit cave in which two snakes, a male and a female, are mating. From the union of these two snakes there continually spring "child seeds"—many of which enter into the shaman's soul, so that henceforth he bears more soul-strength than an ordinary person.'

Other accounts speak of a 'medicine' which the shaman receives in the depths. This medicine is said to look like transparent crystals in which the colours of the rainbow shine. These magical crystals are called *alumburru* and enter into the shaman's body through the cavity beside the collarbone or through the navel or penis. The strength conveyed by Ugud resides in the man's abdomen. A man whose soul has been endowed with special strength by the snake henceforth feels a radiant light and a great brightness within him.

An old man gave the following account of the experience of being called: 'The strength enters into the shaman's body through the navel. He plunges into the deep water; a snake at the bottom gives him two eggs that grow in him. When he first comes up out of the water the man is sick and has fever. But the eggs grow in him. It is good if he drinks much water, for then the strength in him drinks water. The water comes out of him again as urine, therefore urine has healing power.'

In their accounts of the experience of being called it is generally only in response to detailed questioning that the aborigines distinguish between the physical and the mental existence of a man who is to become a shaman. Usually they relate how 'he' plunges into the water, receives the medicine, returns to the surface, etc. Only after a precise question does it become clear that the shaman's body lies in a deep sleep with his family, whereas 'he' means the shaman's soul which goes through the experiences in the depths of the earth.

Another account of the experience of being called in northwestern Australia runs: 'Perhaps a man is lying asleep, he is an ordinary man, but in his sleep he suddenly thinks: "Why am I not a shaman? I could become a shaman." He dreams, and his soul leaves him during his sleep and goes away. The soul travels through many countries until it comes to a very deep water-hole at the bottom of which it sees a snake. The soul comes back. The soul says: "My father, come with me, dive with me into the deep water, I have seen something there." The man wakes after such a dream and begins an un-settled wandering life until somewhere or other he finds the water-hole that his soul saw in his dreams. Then he lies down on the edge of this water-hole and falls asleep. In his sleep his soul tries once again to see the snake at the bottom of the water. In his dream his soul dives deep down into the water to the place where it becomes black and dark, and in his dream the shaman feels himself die. But the dead soul dives on until it comes to a cave in which it is dry and bright and in which the sun is shining. In the hole there is a great snake. The soul sits down and the snake speaks to it and gives it "medicine". Thereupon the soul rises to the surface of the water again and comes back. The man wakes and feels that he is alive again. But he is sick and can walk only slowly. Very slowly and laboriously he returns to his family and tells them that he has seen the snake. The people say, "We want to see the snake too", and everyone wanders, guided by the shaman, to the water-hole at which he has had his experience of being called.

'Here the people demand that, to prove he has been called, the new shaman shall dive down into the water and bring back "medicine".

'During this test in Australia the young shaman is supported by an older one who has accompanied him. While the young shaman enters the water-hole and dives down into it, the old shaman throws crystals, which are considered to be medicine, into the air and into the water. The young shaman catches some of the crystals and pretends to have found them at the bottom of the water. When the people see the transparent crystals in the hand of the young medicine man they believe him.

'Thus the older shaman plays the role of initiator while the young one has to undergo something like an initiation. This seems to indicate that in Australia too the figure of the shaman is bound to certain forms, that traditional knowledge is passed on from the older generation to suitable younger men.'

Alongside this very external reflection of a psychological event, however, it appears from the statement of an informant that here, too, by the water-hole, the future shaman undergoes a profound emotional experience that extends to all those present. Evidently the bystanders are put into a trance by the two shamans and feel that psychic power has been conveyed to them.

This experience is described as follows: 'The young shaman dives down into the depths to the snake and says to it: "There are many people standing on the bank, they want to see you." The old shaman follows him, and the two come to the surface with the snake. The two shamans ride on the snake in the water; the people on the bank can only see the snake's head. But the snake scatters crystals around it. After a while it disappears into the depths again. But the two shamans distribute crystals to all those present. Everyone receives some.'

The informant concluded: 'There are people who from their youth have the "medicine", but such people are not strong and they lose the power later. But a shaman who has seen the snake in the depths and obtained medicine never again loses this power. He can always heal the sick.'[40]

THE NATURE OF THE SHAMAN

The shaman's psychic rebirth through overcoming a sickness

All accounts agree that a man cannot escape the compulsion of the spirits which seek to make him a shaman. The demands of the spirits drive the future shaman deeper and deeper into mental confusion and physical illness. In many reported cases this condition becomes altogether grave; if it can be resolved, we are confronted by an experience of death and rebirth that must be taken seriously. If the condition cannot be resolved, the individual lapses into insanity or dies.

The way out of the situation lies in shamanizing; that is to say, the mental sickness can be healed only if the sufferer accepts the often unwanted and feared office of shaman, which the spirits are forcing upon him.

We gain the impression that early man has found an almost unfailing way of curing mental disease, that a certain 'psychic constitution' makes escape from a pathological state possible.

Holm describes a typical example of this mystic experience of rebirth among the Angmagsalik Eskimos:[41]

'The first thing the disciple has to do is to go to a certain lonely spot, an abyss or a cave, and there, having taken a small stone, rub it on the top of a large one the way of the sun. When they have done this for three days on end, they say, a spirit comes out from the rock. It turns its face towards the rising sun and asks what the disciple will. The disciple then dies in the most horrible torments, partly from fear, partly from overstrain; but he comes to life again later in the day.'

Every Angmagsalik shaman has a special bear at his command. This bear 'is much larger than an ordinary bear, but so thin that all its ribs are visible. The time of its acquisition is at the end of the period of probation, and takes place as follows: It swallows the *angakok* (shaman) whole; it then throws him up again bone by bone until the whole skeleton has been collected. The skeleton is then clothed with flesh and comes to life again.'

A similar purely mythological occurrence is the experience of being swallowed by a bear among the Greenlanders. The novice goes out into the solitude, is swallowed by a bear and then resurrected as a new man, different from head to toe—even his bones have been fitted together afresh. It is the conclusion of a process of maturation that is manifested in this mystical experience. Like every transformation (and every parting from the old), this, too, is bound up with pain. Thus the Greenland account says: 'He dies in terrible pain.' Outwardly the novice described generally loses consciousness and swoons. Thus the experience of transformation is a deeply shattering psychological process that goes to the limits of physical endurance.

After the body has been swallowed by the monster a metamorphosis takes place in the novice; he is born bit by bit as a changed, new man. Among the East Greenlanders the novice has to undergo several such rebirths in order to become a good shaman.

Among the Klamath Indians a corresponding process is recounted in the myth of a bear that lives in a great lake. One day a man saw the bear standing upright in the water. 'Here I shall swim,' said the man and dived into the water, whereupon the bear disappeared. Later the man was found by his fellow tribesmen unconscious, and blood came out of his mouth. The bear had caught him and made him a shaman. He 'nearly died' before the spirit had made him a shaman.[42] In this example, too, we have a kind of death and resurrection. Only when the novice had lost consciousness through swimming for a long time in the lake, and had been captured by the bear in his vision, could he become a shaman.

A very interesting account of the experience of dying and rebirth is contained in the autobiography of a Winnebago Indian.[43]

This is particularly revealing because it contains the account of a person who has been through the ceremony himself. 'What I was most eager to see was myself killed and then brought back to life again, in the (medicine) lodge,' says the initiate. This happens in the 'shooting ritual', which constitutes the most important element in the Winnebago Medicine Dance.

'There seems to be little doubt', writes the author of this account, 'that the killing and coming to life again in the shooting ritual was always regarded by the older members of the Medicine Dance as symbolical.' Among the older members the person to be initiated is known as 'he-for-whom-we-desire-life'.[44]

The special experience of being cut in pieces

From Siberia come numerous accounts of the future shaman being cut in pieces by spirits. The shaman is 'boiled'. All the spirits over which he will later have power eat his flesh before putting him together again and resurrecting him.

During this purely psychic experience the shaman lies in a deep swoon. He undergoes an extraordinarily dangerous psychological experience, a process of transformation, the result of which is an increase in his psychic potency. It is a genuine experience of death and rebirth that is always very clearly described in images which remain always the same, but with which it is beyond the power of modern man to identify himself.

The shaman's time of suffering may be so intense as to involve those around him too—indeed, there are accounts in which the 'spirits' have demanded the death of one or more members of the shaman's family and only after these have died has the shaman come into his full powers.

'The shamans are born in the far north, at the source of the terrible sicknesses.' Here stands a larch on whose branches many nests are attached at various heights. The greatest shamans are trained at the top of the great tree, the middle ones half-way up, the little shamans on the lower branches.

It is said that first a large bird, like an eagle with iron feathers, flies to this tree, perches on it, and lays an egg. Then this bird hatches the egg. If a very great shaman is to emerge from it the bird hatches it for three years; if a small shaman for one year.

The bird is called 'Mother of Animals' and shows herself on three occasions: the first, when she gives birth to a shaman; the second, when his development is terminated by the cutting up of his body; the third, when the shaman is dying.

When the shaman—his soul—crawls out of the egg this bird gives him a spirit shamaness by name Bürgestey-Udagan, who has one leg, one hand, and one eye. This shamaness puts the shaman to bed in an iron cradle, rocks him, and brings him up on pieces of coagulated blood.

When the upbringing in the cradle is finished the future shaman is handed over to three black, gaunt spirits who hack his flesh in pieces. First they put the shaman's head on a pole. Then they scatter the hacked-up flesh in all directions like an offering. While this is being done three other spirits throw the shaman's jawbone as an oracle for the origins of all afflictions and diseases. If the oracle bone falls in the normal position, this means that the shaman can save mankind from the illness in question. It is said that sometimes the shaman's flesh is not sufficient for all sufferings and ailments. Then he is permitted to shamanize once only for each of those maladies that could not be provided for by a piece of his flesh.

Two years ago in the summer a man said he had soon to become a shaman. He ordered a hut to be built for him in the forest close to a clearing. The hut was built beside the tallest larch, on which hung a multitude of shamanistic idols that were kept there after the seance. Young, still unmarried boys had to build it, according to his instructions, of unpeeled logs. This man's name was Mikhail Savvich Nikitin. He was about 40 years old.

He then moved into his hut and lay there for three days. He said: 'I shall lie there like a dead man and shall be cut up (by spirits). On the third day I must rise from the dead.' For this day he commanded a shaman named Bötshükkä to fetch the son of Taapyn, so that he might perform over him the ceremony of the 'raising of the body' and of 'instruction and dedication'.

A future shamaness is reported to have said: 'The time has come when they will cut open my body. In three days I shall die and then rise from the dead. Then wrap my body in birch bark.' A spirit is said to have collected the bones of the shamans and laid them on a peeled birch bark. Then life returned to the bodies and they arose. And again in another variant the words of a future shaman ran: 'When the time of my resurrection [the word could also be translated 'bringing back to life'] approaches gather pure, chaste girls and youths and let them perform the ceremony of my rising from the dead.'

Before anyone can become a shaman, he must be ill. Then he is cut up three times.

I have never yet heard of the shaman being laid on fresh birch bark in this connexion.

In what the Yakuts call 'the old time', a great shaman had of necessity to submit to his body being cut up. While his body was being taken to pieces the shaman had to lie outside his house in the open on freshly peeled birch bark. None of his relatives were allowed to visit the spot. He chose one person only from among his relations to look after him during his illness—a pure boy or a pure girl without sexual experience.

For a full four or five days the shaman lay insensible; white froth flowed copiously from his mouth; from all his joints trickled blood. His whole body was covered with blue patches suffused with blood. He is said to have lost the power of speech. He lay half dead and barely breathed. People would tell one another that in the underworld the shaman's flesh had been separated from his bones and its parts distributed on various paths. A piece went along every branch of the path.

When a shaman's body is cut up he lies for seven days in a swoon. He eats and drinks nothing. Slime is said to flow continuously from all his joints and from both eyes. 'If my body is cut in pieces, then all the pieces are distributed along all the paths of misfortune and affliction.' So the shamans themselves say. The events that take place during this period are described very well in the accounts of shamans from among the Buryat; again and again they show clearly that the future shaman is in a situation from which there is no escape except to become a shaman.

Before a man becomes a shaman he is sick for a long time. It seems to him that the souls of dead shamans, his *ucha* (ancestors), come and teach him. When these ancestors come the novice becomes abstracted; he speaks to them as to the living. None of those not participating can see them. Sometimes one comes, sometimes a few, sometimes many, almost all dead shamans.

'All these shamans torment me, beat me, cut off my flesh with knives, throw it about, stab me in the stomach and demand that I become a shaman.'

While the ancestors are stabbing and cutting, the shaman himself lies half dead. His heart can scarcely be heard beating, his breathing is weak, his hands and face turn dark blue.

'Then you come to life again, your fingers begin to move, you breathe more and more deeply.'

When the souls of the dead shamanistic ancestors have instructed the Buryat novice, whom they are forcing to become a shaman, in heaven, they boil him so that he shall become ready [mature, properly cooked]. In antiquity all shamans were boiled, so that they should learn the shamanistic knowledge. While this is going on he lies for seven days as though dead. Then his family sing: 'Our shaman will come back to life, he will set us free!' The spirits of his shamanistic ancestors say to him: 'Now we shall cut off your flesh, that you may be perfect. But we shall put the flesh back again, and you will come back to life and be a shaman.' So they did.

The Tungus say of their shamans: 'Before a man becomes a shaman he is sick for a long time. His understanding becomes confused. The shamanistic ancestors of his clan come, hack him to bits, tear him apart, cut his flesh in pieces, drink his blood. They cut off his head and throw it in the oven, in which various iron appurtenances of his costume are made red-hot and then forged. This cutting up is carried out somewhere in the upper world by the shaman ancestors. He alone receives the gift of shamanhood who has shaman ancestors in his clan who pass it on from generation to generation; and only when these have cut up his body and examined his bones can he begin to shamanize.'

The shaman Timofey relates: 'When I was fifteen I fell ill. My shamanistic ancestors compelled me to follow the path of shamanistic service. When I began to sing, the sickness usually passed temporarily. Then my ancestors shamanized. They set me up like a stake and shot at me with bows until I lost consciousness. They cut up my flesh, took out the bones and counted them. When they had counted my bones, they noticed that there were too many. If there had not been enough bones, I could not have become a shaman.'

The soul of the future shaman among the Yakuts is dragged by his shaman ancestors (chiefly on his mother's side) into the subterranean world and there held imprisoned for one to three years, being taught and educated. After the passage of a certain time they have to cut the future shaman's 'body' into pieces.

The shamans themselves usually relate: 'They cut off the head and place it on the topmost beam of the Yakut *yurta*; they cut off all the extremities, but they chop up the flesh and distribute it among all kinds of corruption and death.

'They cut off the head and place it on the uppermost plank in the *yurta*, from where it watches the chopping up of its body. They hook an iron hook into the body and tear up and distribute all the joints; they clean the bones, by scratching off the flesh and removing all the fluid. They take the two eyes out of the sockets and put them on one side. The flesh removed from the bones is scattered on all the paths in the underworld; they also say that it is distributed among the nine or three times nine generations of the spirits which cause sickness, whose roads and paths the shaman will in future know. He will be able to help with ailments caused by them; but he will not be able to cure those maladies caused by spirits that did not eat of his flesh.'

The shaman's bones are counted by the spirits to see whether they are all there. If a bone is missing, one of the shaman's closest blood relations must die. Another version states that during the development of a great shaman as many of his blood relations must die as he has main bones in his body. These dead give him the possibility of becoming a shaman. According to yet other statements by natives, in olden times a shaman's whole family died during his initiation; for every one of the shaman's bones the spirits demanded a ransom from among his family: for eight long bones eight people, for the skull one. For the ten main bones ten people died. The shaman who was cut up in due order did not come back to life without a human ransom.

The old people say of the shaman's healing power: 'He helps on condition that the source of a particular illness, the evil spirit, has received his share, a part of his flesh. When a great shaman comes into being, his family dies out. The spirits make use of his dying relatives as bars of the weir that is built across the river. Chosen shamans must have water from the river of death.'

The shamans themselves say that the body of a great shaman is cut up three times, that of a small shaman once. During this time he is said to lie fighting with death. They say that during this time the spirits gather. When the body is cut up they take off his head and put it on top of a stake. But they cut up his flesh into small pieces and share it

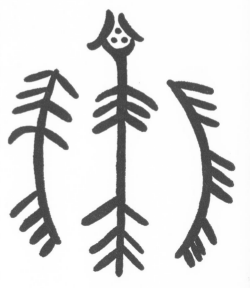

Drawing of a shaman's skeleton on a Siberian shaman's drum

out among all those present. . . . There are said to be an enormous number of them. If one of them eats flesh from the legs, the shaman will heal diseases of the legs. If one of them eats flesh from the ears, the shaman will heal diseases of the ears. If the parts of the body are not sufficient for all the spirits, the shaman is not allowed to shamanize. He can overcome only those spirits which have eaten of his flesh. Those people who are preparing themselves for the shaman's vocation, but who then abandon this idea, usually say: 'My bones were too few. Therefore the spirits turned round.'

Being cut in pieces means, in effect, dying and being resurrected. During the period of initiation of the great shamans in earlier times seven of his fellow clansmen were said to die.

To begin with, the future shaman falls ill for a long period. He is seized by fits of convulsive singing. The spirits who enter into him are singing. The sickness lasts for varying periods, sometimes as long as five or six years. The spirits of his forefathers, long-dead shamans, descend. The spirit of a dead shaman who has no blood relations becomes a wandering spirit. Sometimes a spirit of this kind finds an unhappy man just when he is singing.

When there are blood-related descendants, the shaman spirit descends for choice

Eskimo drawing of a spirit. Kigutiliq or the Spirit with the Gigantic Teeth. One day, when the artist was hunting seals, this monster rose from a hole in the ice. He was so frightened that he fled home without having taken the monster to be his helping spirit.

upon descendants in the female line. Of the famous shamans of the past, so far as is known, only one, the shaman Küstekh, did not descend upon a member of his daughter's family. In the case of many who are called, almost all their closer relatives perish. The spirit of the shaman ancestor kills them, destroys them, eats them, because his descendant opposes his call.

In the case of a great shaman, one person from among his blood relations has to die for every bone of his body, as a ransom: for the eight long bones, eight people; for the skull, one person. Thus nine people die for the nine chief bones.

This rule, that a shaman who has been cut up in due order does not return to life without a human ransom, has since ancient times become incorporated in a phrase often used in speaking of a shaman. We say: 'That is a great, a terrible man whose name must not be taken in vain in the consecrated month.'

With such a shaman one must never quarrel. Nor should one contradict him. He must be given everything he asks for, and all his commands must be carried out. Otherwise he can provoke any disaster.

Before men become shamans they are ill for a long time. They grow thin, are nothing but skin and bone. They go out of their minds, talk meaningless nonsense, keep on climbing up into the tops of larch trees. And all the time they talk rubbish, as though their eyes were being put out, their bodies being cut up, as though they were being taken to pieces and eaten, as though new blood were being poured into them and so on. People say that during this time the shaman's face becomes quite bloody. When a shaman of the light spirits comes into existence his clan becomes rich. But when a maleficent shaman comes into being eight people of his clan die for his eight long bones.

They say that when a shaman appears people of his clan must die. I have also heard stories of a weir that the shaman builds with his vertebrae. 'When a new shaman is born who has greater powers than the others, this new shaman tears down the weir when he appears.'[45]

The helping spirits in the shape of animals

At the end of a long series of psychological experiences extending, perhaps, over several years there comes a sudden moment, an illumination, a breakthrough, which turns the aspirant into a fully fledged shaman.

But there are also instances where one such experience alone—perhaps a sudden shock—is enough to bring about this metamorphosis and transform a normal man, whose predisposition for shamanhood had passed unnoticed, into a shaman.

In many accounts—above all from among the Eskimos—the result of the long and painful period of preparation is seen as the acquisition of increased psychic power through the shaman's command of 'helping spirits'. Helping spirits in various, generally fantastic shapes or in the form of exceptionally large animals show themselves to the shaman in visions and place themselves at his command. He can call them whenever he wishes.

The concept of the 'helping spirits' is naturally difficult for modern man to under-stand. It is an image that stands for a definite psychological event—an increase in psychic power. Although the event is purely psychological, there is no reason to doubt the reality of this psychic development, the increase in power. This development, the process of acquiring helping spirits, is described in a very similar manner by many groups belonging to hunting cultures in very different regions.

'Although everything was ready for me while I was still in my mother's belly, I tried in vain to become a conjurer up of spirits with the help of others. I never succeeded. I visited many famous shamans and gave them large presents, which they immediately passed on to other people. For if they had kept them for themselves, their children would have died. Then I went out into the solitude and soon became very melancholy. In a mystical fashion I used to break out in complaints and become unhappy, without knowing the reason. Then sometimes everything would suddenly become quite different and I felt a great and inexplicable joy, a joy so strong that I could not control it. I had to break into song, into a mighty song that had no room for anything but this word: Joy! Joy! Joy! And in the midst of this mysterious bliss I became a shaman, without

Drawing of a shaman with rays coming out of his head. From a shaman's drum, Siberia

knowing how. But I was a shaman, I could see and hear in an entirely new way.

'Every real shaman has to feel an illumination in his body, in the inside of his head or in his brain, something that gleams like fire, that gives him the power to see with closed eyes into the darkness, into the hidden things or into the future, or into the secrets of another man. I felt that I was in possession of this marvellous ability.

'My first helping spirit became my name, a little *aua*. When it came to me, it was as if the door and roof rose and I received such power of vision that I could see right through the house, into the earth and up into the sky. It was the little *aua* that brought me all this inner light, by soaring over me so long as I sang. Then it stood outside in a corner of the doorway, invisible to everyone, but always ready when I called it.

'An *aua* is a little spirit, a woman, who lives down on the shore. There are many of these shore spirits. They run about with pointed skin caps on their heads, their trousers are quaintly short and of bearskin. They have high boots with black pattens and furs of sealskin. Their feet are turned upwards and they seem to walk only on their heels. They hold their hands with the thumbs always pressed against the palms. They hold their arms raised with folded hands, as though they were continuously stroking their heads. They are gay and jolly when you call them, and look most like small, charming, living dolls, for when standing up straight they are no taller than an arm's length.

'A shark became my second helping spirit. One day I was out in my kayak when it came swimming up to me, turned over on its side and whispered my name. I was very surprised, because I had never seen a shark before. They are very rare up here. After that it helped me with every kind of hunt and was always with me when I needed it.

'These two, shore spirit and shark, were my most important helping spirits and they helped me with everything I wished. The song I used to sing when I called them did not have many words and went like this:

> Joy! Joy!
> Joy! Joy!
> I see the little shore spirit,
> My name.
> Joy! Joy!

I could repeat these words over and over again, until finally I burst into tears, the prey to a strange fear.

'Then I could suddenly shiver all over my body, as I shouted out again:

> A—a—a—ah!
> Joy! Joy!
> Now I want to go home.
> Joy! Joy!

'Once I had lost a son, and I thought I should never again be able to leave the spot at which I had buried his body. I was just like a mountain spirit that is afraid of human beings. We remained for a very long time in the interior of the land, and my helping spirits left me. But one day the song of joy suddenly came back to me. I longed for people again, my helping spirits returned to me. I was myself again. Since that day I always sing the song when I call them.'[46]

All these myths, of course, are concerned with the description of a psychological experience, a process whose end result is the acquisition of increased psychic force. The experience is seen as the support of the shaman by spirits in the shape of animals. The description of this experience in the myths is by no means clearly intelligible; we can neither understand nor repeat the experience and must try to approach the essence of it by assembling quotations.

Arthur Waley collected shamanistic odes dating from the fourth to the third century B.C.[47] These shamanistic odes already reflect a shamanism that has been filtered through a highly developed culture. Here the helping spirits no longer have the form of animals, but are 'gods' who take possession of the shaman. The shaman's relation to the spirit is represented as a kind of love affair.

Waley continues:

'It is clear at any rate that the relation between the shaman and the deity is a fleeting one, and perhaps the closest analogy to it may be found in the situation of the *hito-toki joro* (single-time concubines) chosen as temporary consorts for the visiting god at the time of certain Shintō festivals in Japan. Some *mikro* (shaman) songs in the twelfth-century Japanese collection *Ryojin Hissho* show the god clearly as a lover. For example:

Kami naraba	If you are a god
Yurara-sarara-to	With a swing and a swish
Ori-tamae!	Deign to come down
Ikanaru kami ka	Would any god
Monohaji wo suru?	Be shy about such matters?

'In the *Nine Songs* the typical form is this: first the shaman (a man if the deity is female, a girl if the deity is male) sees the Spirit descending and goes out to meet it, riding in an equipage drawn by strange or mythical creatures. In the next part of the song the shaman's meeting with the Spirit (a sort of romantic honeymoon) is over. The Spirit has proved fickle and the shaman wanders about love-lorn, waiting in vain for the lover's return. Between these two parts may have come the shaman's main ecstatic dance.'

Waley also comments that so far as he knows this notion of a love affair between a shaman and a spirit does not exist in the classical shamanistic areas—Siberia, Manchuria, Central Asia. But this is incorrect. A whole series of reports indicates that the possession of a shaman by a spirit, his helping spirit or a 'god', assumes precisely the character of such a relationship. The shaman's artistic productivity, his power of conviction and his psychological transformation, which does not permit him to doubt the reality of his psychic experiences, rest upon hysterical components.

The shaman's change of sex, described by numerous anthropologists—when women feel themselves to be men and men feel themselves to be women—also springs from the psychological intensity of sexual experiences. Such experiences naturally occur in China in what one might call a more sublimated stage and not in quite the same form as in an aboriginal shamanism, where the helping spirit is simply felt to be a zoomorphic being.

Among the Siberian peoples, as among the Eskimos, the spirit which supports the shaman most often appears in the shape of an animal. The animals that appear most frequently are wolves, bears, ravens, seagulls and eagles. Jochelson reports that among the Koryak he met a shaman to whom the spirits appeared in the solitary wastes sometimes in human shape and sometimes in the shape of animals, and ordered him to become a shaman or die.

The Yakut speak of a shaman's 'animal mother', a spirit being that cares for him from birth, fosters his development and supports him. Only great shamans have such 'mothers', smaller ones have to be content with helping spirits in the shape of dogs. The Russian anthropologist G. V. Ksenofontov has collected a series of myths from the Yakut, Buryat and Tungus dealing with the activities of the animal mothers and helping spirits.

The following are a selection from the accounts gathered by Ksenofontov:

Only a great shaman, it is said, has an 'animal mother'. Small shamans perform their duties with the aid of unimportant injurious spirits, with *üör* of local origin.

The animal mother comes at the birth and during the time of the education of the shaman's soul; she returns again later only at his death. If the animal mother has reappeared and shown herself to the shaman, this is regarded as an omen of his death. All shamanistic animal mothers, it is said, look very alike and have similar characteristics.

The animal mother of a great shaman has the appearance of a great elk, that of a small shaman the appearance of a reindeer. She comes when the shaman is dying and carries away his cervical vertebrae in her teeth.

They say the shaman has specially strong vision; he can see in all directions. This power of vision, the 'fire of the eyes', extends over greater distances in a great shaman than in a small one.

Every shaman must have an animal mother or an animal of origin. This is mostly envisaged in the shape of an elk, more rarely that of a bear. This animal goes about entirely on its own, separate from the shaman. It is perhaps best pictured as the fiery power of the shamanistic sight, which hastens about the earth. [It is the embodiment of the shaman's prophetic gift, his power of sight, which penetrates into past and future. G.V.K.] This animal mother comes at the moment of the shaman's death.

The animal mother of a Tungus shaman, many people say, has the appearance of a mountain deer with a bare skin, with eight legs growing from the front part of the trunk and with its hoofs turned backwards, or she looks like a female elk or like a bear.

According to tradition, every shaman has a so-called 'animal mother'. She is said to have the appearance of a large bird with a beak that is reminiscent of an iron icebreaker, with hooklike climbing-claws and a tail three swinging-threads in length.

The animal mother, according to many Siberian accounts, begins to give her aid very early on. The shaman's soul is abducted by the animal mother and brought up in a nest on a tree. The significance of this idea is not clear, impressive as are the tales told about it. The soul of a future shaman is born at the foot of a mountain called Jokuo. Here there grows a large fir tree with its top broken or chopped off and branches that are turned downwards. Every branch and twig of this tree, from the lowest to the topmost, bears birds' nests. The shamans of the whole world are brought up on this one tree. The greater the shaman in importance and power, the higher in the tree dwells his soul, that is to say, the souls dwell at various heights. The shamans themselves usually say that a raven appears as teacher, which sits on the branches of this tree and educates the souls.

The shamans whose souls are brought up in the nests on the upper branches become stronger and more important than those brought up in the lower nests. The nests are attached in regular rows and rise step by step with the space of one branch between one row and the next.

First the future shaman becomes mentally deranged, some at the age of nine, others as early as seven. The mental illness lasts from three to seven years. Others fall mentally ill as adults. The sufferer alternates between attacks and periods of lucidity.

In the sky there is a tree named Yjyk-Mas. Its top reaches up into the ninth heaven. No one can ascertain its circumference. From its root to its tip, this tree is covered with excrescences. No branch is free from them. In these excrescences the shamans are born, the shamanesses and all those familiar with magic and witchcraft. The strong ones are born at the foot of the tree. Shamans with full powers are born in an excrescence that is as big as a small grave mound.

But people also say that the greatest shamans are brought up in the underworld among the evil spirits, the spirits of conflict and mischief, and rocked in a special cradle. Down there lives a smith, Kydai-Bakhsy. In his smithy both smiths and shamans are welded together and tempered. The great and terrible shamans spring from this source.

People say that there is a special tree, called the Aar-Kuduk-Mas, the great, the sacred tree. On the branches of this tree there are many nests like those of birds in which the souls of shamans are brought up. The nests are attached to the tree from the top to the bottom.

When shamans quarrel with each other they try first to destroy their adversary's nest. He who first succeeds in doing this emerges the victor.[48]

The technique of shamanizing

Shamanizing begins with the shaman putting himself in a trance by various means, chiefly by monotonous, repetitive sounds produced by a drum or rattle, and by dancing movements. Consciousness is eliminated and the productive subconscious levels of the mind find expression. Not only does this enable the shaman's power of artistic creation to work upon his audience by presenting the image of the community's vision of the world to the consciousness of the spectators, the listeners, the sick and the mentally disturbed. It seems also that in a state of trance the shaman is able to transfer on to the others, better or more lastingly, the power of healing which he has gained for himself.

The shaman always operates in a state of trance.

He voluntarily puts himself in this state, in which his unconscious power of image-making speaks and through which he enables the others to participate in this act of creation.

The new powers which he has acquired through shamanizing may be transmitted to others, or else similar powers are aroused in them.

The mentally sick person heals himself by functioning first not as a priest and doctor but as an artist. He gives artistic form to his inner images, composes poetry, dances, mimes, and so on.

The trance, the process of giving shape to inner images, is experienced by the shaman as communication with spirits; the displacement of the level of consciousness is seen as a 'journey' into the 'beyond'. The 'spirits' and the 'journey' are never conceived of as phenomena of the shaman's own mind. The spirits are presumed to speak through the shaman to the community, to bestow good hunting and health. On the journey undertaken by his soul, while his body lies 'like dead', the shaman is able to visit 'distant lands', the 'beyond', the 'gods', or the 'underworld', and to bring back important information.

It seems, therefore, that what we have here is a special psychological technique. Communication with the 'spirits' seems to be an activation of levels of the mind not available to these people—or to anyone—in full consciousness. It is evidently a very ancient technique which is not yet accessible to modern psychology, but which represents a means of curing certain depressive states, based on thousands of years of experience. The essence of this process of self-healing consists in imposing order and form upon these confused and chaotic images, which threaten to overwhelm the individual.

The content of experience during this process, according to all reports, is very similar over wide areas.

Radloff describes the state of excitement into which a Siberian shaman puts himself by dancing, and of which he was an eyewitness, as follows: 'Some shamans dance so wildly that in the end they sink down as though dead; others get into such a violent ecstasy that they have to be held fast and bound, which can be done only by several men exerting all their strength. Then the bound shaman often trembles and twitches for a long time and tries to twist himself free, until the drum falls from his hands and he lies for hours as though dead.'[49]

Mikhailovskii also gives a good description of an ecstatic state, this time from among the Buryat. 'The longer the action continues, the stronger will be the inspiration.'[50]

An example in which possession by an animal spirit is manifested—for example by the spirit of a wolf—is given by Jochelson, who witnessed a shamanistic performance among the Koryak: 'Suddenly the shaman commenced to beat the drum softly and to sing in a plaintive voice; then the beating of the drum grew stronger and stronger, and his song—in which could be heard sounds imitating the howling of the wolf, the groaning of the cargoose, and the voices of the other animals, his guardian spirits— appeared to come, sometimes from the corner nearest to my seat, then from the opposite end, then again from the middle of the house, and then it seemed to proceed from the ceiling . . . The wild fits of ecstasy which would possess him during his performance frightened me.'[51]

A detailed description of a Yakut shamanistic performance, in which the shaman goes into an ecstasy and is possessed by a spirit, is presented by Czaplicka after Siero-

14   *Wooden doll forming part of a shaman's equipment. North-west America*

15 *A shaman dancing with spirits. Turkish painting*

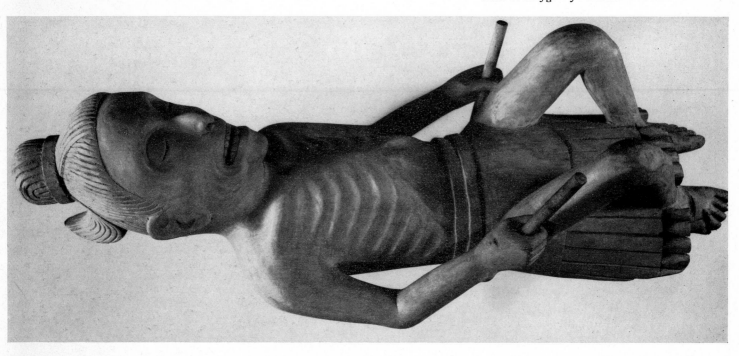

16 *Small wooden figure of a dead shaman. North-west America*

szewski: 'Only the gentle sound of the voice of the drum, like the humming of a gnat, announces that the shaman has begun to play . . . The audience scarcely breathes, and only the unintelligible mutterings and hiccoughs of the shaman can be heard; gradually even this sinks into a profound silence. Then the music grows louder and louder and, like peals of thunder, wild shouts rend the air; the crow calls, the grebe laughs, the seamews complain, snipes whistle, eagles and hawks scream. The music swells and rises to the highest pitch. The numberless small bells (on the shaman's garment) ring and clang . . . It is a whole cascade of sounds, enough to overwhelm all the listeners . . . Then sombrely the voice of the shaman chants the following obscure fragments:

> Mighty bull of the earth . . . Horse of the steppes!
> I, the mighty bull, bellow!
> I, the horse of the steppes, neigh!
> I, the man set above all other beings!

'In the ensuing prayers the shaman addresses his *ämägyat* and other protective spirits; he talks with the *kaliany*, asks them questions, and gives answers in their names. Sometimes the shaman must pray and beat the drum a long time before the spirits come; often their appearance is so sudden and so impetuous that the shaman is overcome and falls down.

'When the *ämägyat* comes down to a shaman, he arises and begins to leap and dance . . . and beats the drum uninterruptedly . . . Those who hold him by the leather thongs (he is bound) sometimes have great difficulty in controlling his movements. The head of the shaman is bowed, his eyes are half-closed; his hair is tumbled and in wild disorder lies on his sweating face, his mouth is twisted strangely, saliva streams down his chin, often he foams at the mouth.'[52]

Further descriptions of the shaman's abnormal state while shamanizing are to be found in Jochelson[53] and Schirokogorow.[54]

The shaman's psychological experiences during the ecstasy are generally pictured as a journey into the land of souls, the beyond, the underworld or the sky or over wide geographical areas—real, known regions. Similar psychic experiences must underlie these accounts of travel, which are astonishingly alike from Siberia and North America to Australia.

Also common to all these regions is the fact that the inner experiences are so intense that they are unquestioningly taken for outside 'real' events and described as such.

The power of suggestion of these experiences and their artistic formulation is so great that the bystanders often participate in them.[55]

Stick with handle in the shape of a horse's head, a primitive stringed instrument used by the shaman on his journey to the next world. Buryat, Siberia

The nature of the shaman—a provisional definition

Thus shamanism is not, as is often supposed, a religion, but a psychological technique which, theoretically, could appear within the framework of any religion. But shamanism seems to emerge essentially within primitive religions and here above all as part of the religious ideas of the hunting peoples.

Shamanism springs from an intensification of the ego-potency at a time when man was by no means master of his environment but at the mercy of the overwhelming forces of nature.

Shamanism is a first attempt to subdivide the environment into matter and spirit and achieve a spiritual efficacy. Painted animals are therefore 'spirit animals' and not copies of real animals.

The psychological technique of shamanism consists in operating with fixed notions and playing them off against one another; that is to say, not in an intellectual manner but on the psychological plane, a technique which is still alien to modern psychology; the method consists more or less in making obsessional ideas conscious and thus dissolving them. Shamanism is a technique in which imaginings are transposed into images and then played off against one another.

All the images, in conformity with the hunter's view of the world, are images of animals. All conflicts and struggles are experienced and portrayed as struggles with and between animals.

The development of the shaman from an initial illness to the overcoming of this illness is also seen in the form of animal entities which first persecute and then aid him.

It is through this preoccupation with the animal world that the numerous depictions of animals in cave paintings are linked with shamanism.

The art of shamanism, as is only to be expected of hunters' art, consists almost exclusively of representations of animals. To be regarded as having a special connexion with shamanism are, on the one hand, portrayals of animals fighting, and, on the other, the so-called X-ray style. In the X-ray style vital internal organs of animals are depicted. To shamanism belongs the concept of the resuscitation of animals out of body-parts, bones, and so on. This idea of resuscitation is attached to certain supposedly magical crystallization points: the skulls and thigh-bones of the early hunters, in the case of animals also pieces of skin, by means of which the animal can bring itself back to life or be brought back to life by others. We may wonder whether the so-called tree burial is not connected with this, since there are indications that among the Eskimos bodies

Engraved bone from southern France (Magdalenian). Men in two rows, head, spine and front legs of a bison; probably the portrayal of a resuscitation ritual

are disposed of in this way not merely to protect the bones from wild animals but because the skeleton is to be brought closer to life through 'the air'.

Hunting magic largely consists in hunting, catching, and killing the souls of animals, actions which are thought then to be almost automatically transferred to the bodies of the animals.

Fertility is guaranteed by preserving and sacrificing parts of animals' bodies to which the soul is attached. The soul is sent back on the assumption that it will then 're-embody' itself, so that it can be hunted afresh.

The shaman's trance technique is based on the theoretical supposition that the human soul can be separated from the body. While separated from the body, the soul can be sent out to far places or other worlds, and then recalled.

The earliest evidence of this conception of the possibility of dividing a living being into a soul or 'picture' and a body is to be found in the ceremonial burial of bears' skulls.

THE FUNCTION OF THE SHAMAN

His position in the community

There is no proof that primitive man was healthy, or healthier than civilized man, and above all we must realize that primitive man is quite exceptionally susceptible to various forms of mental disorder. Psychoses, neuroses, hallucinations, mass hysteria and the like are of very frequent occurrence. The shaman can cure these states—but only when he has overcome them in himself.

Where shamans exist, they are the centre of the native community. Irrespective of whether it is a smaller or a larger community, it is always grouped round one or several shamans.

Naturally these groups are always comparatively small—twenty to thirty people, at the very outside 300. Hunters always live in small groups, which wander over a relatively large area. The food supply of such a group, the animals it hunts, can only live spread out over a wide area.

The economic life of hunters does not permit them to feed a larger number of people. If shamanism is to be regarded as a form of religion, it is the form practised by small groups. A shaman's influence, which has to be exercised without apparatus, without writing, without a regular 'ecclesiastical life', can only reach a small group. Even if the shaman's personality is very strong and his reputation so widespread that people with no shaman in their vicinity travel long distances to see him, the circle or group which forms around him nevertheless always remains comparatively small.

Such a group of natives must be regarded not as a sum of individuals, but rather as a total organism, whose limbs consist of individuals. The individual human being cannot live without a collective of this kind.

The shaman is the centre, the brain, and the soul of such a community. He is, so to speak, the regulator of the soul of the group or tribe, and his function is to adjust, avert and heal defects, vacillations, disturbances, and diseases of this soul. Looked at biologically, the whole life of primitive people is more strongly influenced by the subconscious than seems to be the case among ourselves. It is clear that in this situation the position of the shaman is one of paramount importance.

Even natural processes, such as human procreation, often need stimulation, animation of the psychological components by the shaman, as is demonstrated by a Yakut story or investigations of conditions among the Australian aborigines.

The shaman's fertility magic

In olden times, according to the stories told by the shamans, a special rite was performed beseeching the spirit of the earth to fill the women with *jalyn*, the energy of the sexual urge. This rite was carried out in conjunction with several *yurta*-owners living in the same summer encampment. The participants would discuss the ceremony at great length while preparing for it. Food was gathered together for the entertainment of the people and special preparations were made.

At a certain time the people assembled. The shaman who had been called also came. A shaman whose guardian spirits were bloodthirsty and evil could not perform this rite. On his journey to the Earthmother the shaman was accompanied by three times nine maidens and the same number of youths. These virgins and youths carried birch branches and danced with the shaman. The shaman put on his robe and also had his drum with him. During the seance he went dancing to the Earthmother and asked her to bestow *jalyn*. Then he received from the Earthmother *jalyn*, sexual passion. With the drum and the drumstick in his hand he began to neigh like a horse and turn around in a circle, shouting '*Khoruu, khoruu!*' as though calling a herd of horses.

At this moment the assembled women broke out into loud cries and began to whinny like mares: '*Innä-sasakh!*' Whinnying, they hurled themselves on the shaman and performed wildly erotic movements of the body over him. They are said even to have thrown him on the ground. The men who were standing by had to beat off the women and drag the shaman free. The shaman rose, gave a whistle, and described circles with his drumstick. Thereupon the women immediately came to themselves, grew calmer and sat down. It is said that while this was going on the women used to break into a sweat and their faces became copper-red with the suffusion of blood.

Three times the shaman performed this rite, each time with the same accompanying circumstances. We hear that the excited women actually threw themselves on the shaman completely naked.

This rite is also called 'the taking of sexual passion from the spirit of the earth for men and beasts' or 'the bringing down of the power of procreation'.[56]

The procreation of the Australian aborigines, for example, diminishes or ceases altogether if their unconscious mental life is disturbed. Far more than among ourselves, their biological productivity seems also to be dependent upon their mental balance.

Disturbances of the subconscious have the effect of reducing the number of children. The aborigines express the inadequate mental disposition to procreation by saying: 'We cannot dream any more children.'

Only the shaman can rectify disturbances of the subconscious, and he only so long as his own mental life is completely unshaken. The effects of European civilization need not yet be evident in a materially tangible form—tales and reports from the domain of white civilization may bring chaos to the hypersensitive mental equilibrium of a shaman.

The occasional sight of an aeroplane flying over the natives' district can produce devastating disturbances among them. All medicine men believe that their souls can leave them in a dream and fly to distant countries. The sight of an aeroplane, which they believe to be the materialized soul of another great and mighty shaman, fills them with fear and feelings of inferiority. A group of aborigines might be compared to a termite state. A termite state is an organism whose limbs are the individual insects. The life of such a termite state ceases if the queen is removed. Similarly life is extinguished among the aborigines if they lose their shaman or he loses his powers.

Then the people either succeed in finding a new shaman or they try to join a group that has a shaman.

Without a shaman, in any case, total degeneration sets in.

The shaman is contemporary man's living link with primeval times and the creation.

Primitive peoples generally have little conception of the future; they live solely in the present and the past, that is to say primeval times. Life in the present is possible only through continual contact with the primeval past. Life in the present is built up as an everlasting repetition of processes that took place in this primeval past. The symbol of the primeval past is the shaman; he does not only live in the present, but in him the creative forces which were active in the primeval past are still alive; he lives, as it were, in a continual dream state.

The shaman thus repeats today everything which the beings of primeval antiquity did during the creation.

As the bearer of soul-force, the shaman is able to cure illnesses.

Through his knowledge of countless magic formulas and rites, he can bewitch objectionable members of the tribe or outside enemies with sicknesses, or kill them. His contact with Ungud, the soul-force of the world, makes it possible for him to separate his soul from his body and fly across vast distances and so find out what is going on in other parts of the world. The shaman is also the only person who can, without danger, have dealings with the wild spirits who eat corpses and abduct the souls of men. He can stay with them as a guest and learn their language and their songs. He is the poet, actor, and producer.

Finally, it is also the shaman who can send his soul down to the dead in the underworld and so maintain contact between the living and their ancestors.

A shaman does not always combine all these abilities in himself. Thus there are many who have some healing powers but no other importance. Others again have the power to send their souls to the spirits or to the underworld and there learn songs. Such men are poets, and their powers generally go no further than that. In the opinion of the natives, every man can exercise a healing influence on others by means of the soul-force, which he carries within him and which he can cause to flow into others through bodily contact.

A real and great shaman will generally possess this measure of power from birth. But he also possesses more. Behind him is felt the might of special mental experiences, which can easily be distinguished from any sham or mere self-importance. Such people are not frequent, and a tribe produces a real shaman only from time to time, and this

figure then unites in himself the tribe's whole mental life. The special powers he possesses are his from birth. They cannot be learned.[57]

Amongst almost all primitive peoples of the world, the shaman's central position is
attained through a series of psychological experiences, which in turn are extraordinarily
similar all over the world. These experiences, called in anthropological literature the
experiences of the 'call', open up to the shaman new areas of the mind and hence powers
not available to other men.

In considering the shaman, great value has rightly been placed on his social function
as priest and doctor. Insufficient attention, however, has been paid to the shaman's
artistic function and productions. Yet the shaman's artistic activity seems to be the main
factor—less important from the social point of view, perhaps, but more so for the
individual.

The whole process of the shaman's evolution and operation is an artistic one. In
this process the group's mythological and cosmological images are activated and
rendered productive, in a personal variation, by the single mentally sick individual.

The result of self-cure is artistic production and activity. The person of the shaman,
the metamorphosis which takes place in him when he begins to shamanize, and the
result of shamanizing, are a form of artistic productivity. Probably they are the earliest
form of all, and in all likelihood the cave paintings of the Ice Age are the work of
early artists who had undergone the process of transformation into a shaman and were
carrying out the activities which follow upon this transformation.

The shaman's hunting magic

When the game is growing scarce the Greenland shaman visits the Mistress of the
Underworld and the Sea Creatures, who lives on the bed of the sea. He frees her from
the vermin in her hair and in return she sends back to the earth the various animals
that she has been withholding.

'He journeyed to the Mother of the Earth, as she is called, by following the path of
the dead. It was not long before he came to another path which turned off to the left;
he took this path and all his assistant spirits followed him. Finally he heard a loud
roaring: it was the Elv that flowed through the house in which the Mother of the Sea
Creatures lived . . . Then he continued on his way and had to jump over three stones
that were covered with slippery seaweed. He stood helpless, but when his assistant
spirits were across he dared the jump and came over safely. Again he flew on and finally
caught sight of the house in which the Mother of the Sea dwelt. Again he had to jump
over a stream. His assistant spirits said to him: "As soon as you are in the house you
must leap upon the Mother of the Sea, seize her by the hair and wind it round your
right arm; then she will try to throw you into the abyss behind her bed. If she succeeds,
you will be stifled in the darkness . . ." When he (the shaman) was in the house, he
seized the woman by her hair and quickly wound it round his right arm. Her attempt
to throw him backwards on to the bed failed, but she lifted him up so that he felt as
though a chasm were opening up beneath him. Then they wrestled together, but his
assistant spirits came to his aid by striking the woman on the ears and shouting: "Be

calm, he has come to comb your hair and cleanse you from vermin." Then she gave in and said: "I am perishing under the filth of men. The impurity of your transgressions dirties me. Quick, clean my head and comb my hair. When you return, tell the people of your tribe to keep strictly to the regulations of the faith. People make no effort to live life rightly, but their obstinacy comes down to me as dirt and makes me ugly. I should have been glad to send my animals to men, but I had to teach them a lesson and make them think." The dirt which the shaman had picked off the Mistress of the Underworld turned into game; so the purpose of the shaman's journey had been achieved.'[58]

The Mother of the Sea Creatures. Eskimo drawing

Rasmussen also gives another description of the shaman's journey to the Mistress of the Underworld:

Before the great magician the path through the earth down into the sea opens up of its own accord; he goes down it without meeting any obstacles, as though falling through a tube . . . if he comes to the woman's house and finds that a wind-wall has been built in front of it, this means that she is hostile to men. The magician must then immediately throw himself against the wall, knock it down and trample it into the ground. Her house is like an ordinary human house, only the roof is missing—it is open at the top so that from her place by the lamp she can keep an eye on the dwelling-places of men. All kinds of game—common seals, bearded seals, walruses, and whales —are gathered in a dragnet on the right of her lamp, where they lie puffing and blowing; only for the sharks she has another place, and these live in her chamber-pot; that is why sharks taste of urine.

The only obstacle to the shaman's entry is a large dog that lies across the doorway and blocks the path. People say that the Mistress of the Underworld was married to the dog before she was abducted by the stormy petrel. The dog shows its teeth and growls threateningly like a ferocious animal that does not want to be disturbed; often it lies there gnawing at the bones of a man who is still alive; without hesitating or showing fear, the shaman should push the dog aside and leap into the house. Here he meets the father, who grabs hold of him and tries to shut him up with the spirits who are atoning for their sins. He must say promptly: 'I am of flesh and blood.' Then nothing will happen to him. As a sign of her anger, the Mother of the Sea Creatures is sitting with her back to the lamp, with her back to all the animals she would otherwise send up to the shores. Her hair, washed down over her face and eyes, is untidy and dishevelled.

As soon as the shaman enters he should seize her by the shoulders and turn her face to the lamp and to the animals, he should stroke her hair and smooth it in a friendly fashion and say: 'Those up above can no longer help the seals out of the sea by their front flippers.' To this the woman answers: 'Your own sins and the levity of your women with the births (this refers to abortions and the breaking of taboos during pregnancy) are blocking the way.' The shaman must employ all his art in order to pacify her anger. As soon as she has been mollified she picks up the animals and drops them one by one on the ground. An eddying springs up, as though a whirlpool were circling in the house, and the animals vanish into the sea. This means good hunting and plenty.

Now it is time for the magician to return to those waiting for him in the camp. They hear him speeding towards them from far off. The roar of his travelling comes closer and closer; with a mighty 'pu,a' he emerges by his place behind the curtain, as a sea beast that compresses its lungs shoots up out of the depths.

For a moment there is silence; no one must break this silence, until the shaman says: 'Let us hear.' And the shaman continues in the solemn language of the spirits: 'Word will rise up.' And then everyone in the house must confess the infringements of the taboo of which they are guilty. They interrupt one another saying: 'Perhaps it is my fault.' Men and women cry out, filled with the fear of bad hunting and hunger; they begin to confess all the wrong they have done. The name of each person in the house is called out, everyone has to confess; in this way they all learn a great deal of which no one had any inkling. Each one hears the secrets of the other. But in spite of all the sins that come to light the shaman often speaks like an unhappy man who has made a mistake. Again and again he bursts out with the words: 'I am seeking the reasons in things that have not happened, I am talking like a man who knows nothing.' Then it suddenly happens that someone comes out with a secret sin that he wanted to hide, and then the shaman utters a great cry of relief. 'That was it!' Often it is the very young women and men who have sinned and are to blame for the misfortune that has come upon the settle, ment. But if the women are young and step forward weeping, this is always a sign that they are good women. For in confession lies forgiveness. Everyone is filled with a great joy that a disaster has been averted, and they are quite sure that the following day there will be a glut of game.[59]

Comparable accounts, if not so clear, have been reported from Australia. These concern not a journey to the Lord of the Animals but a hunting spell which reaches its climax in a mass trance.

Nevertheless the figure of the Mistress of the Animals is known in Australia, especially northern Australia, under the concept of the so,called Wauwelak Sisters, who go about the land begetting animals and plants and sending them out.

Representations of these Mistresses of the Animals are to be seen in rock,paintings and above all in bark,paintings.

The essential thing, however, is the shaman's performance of the hunting magic. The very existence of the group depends upon it. The time for his intervention has come when hunting has proved fruitless for some considerable time. It happens some, times that even skilled hunters may fail for several days to bring back a kangaroo to the camp, and finally the group's food consists solely of roots or small animals, such as lizards, collected by the women. Then the shaman takes kangaroo bones, which he uses as music,sticks, and in the evening he gathers the men around him. They sing ceaselessly to the beat of the bone music,sticks. The singing is not very fast and between each verse the singers repeat in a particular rhythmic sequence the names of all the species of kangaroo which they know. In the songs the sound of leaping kangaroos is imitated, and the men see before them countless kangaroos springing down the rocky mountains, their paws thudding on the rocks. The shaman tirelessly strikes up fresh songs; gradually the singing becomes wilder and more emphatic, then finally it grows soft and beseeching.

The men gradually go into a trance, but continue singing; others collapse and lie as though stupefied among the singers, unheeded by anyone. When day begins to break and the morning mist lies over the bush the song reaches its climax. At the moment when the sun appears over the horizon it ceases. The hunters rise languidly, gnaw the last remnants of the roots left over from the previous day, and set out on the hunt as usual.

Investigators have been assured that after a nocturnal singsong of this kind the kangaroos come towards the hunters from all sides and do not avoid their spears.[60]

Accounts of shamanistic states are available from quite recent times. They all have two things in common: the relaxed, almost unintended beginning, and the incomprehensible, but for that reason all the more impressive, intensity of the later phases.

The vast majority of these accounts also mention the success of the shaman's activities; that is to say complete tranquillity and confidence in the behaviour of the group.

Thus Rasmussen relates:

'On the third evening of the storm we were solemnly invited to a seance in one of the igloos. The host was a distinctly fair-skinned Eskimo with a bald head, red full beard and eyes that had a slight tendency towards blueness. His name was Kingiuna. The storm seemed now to have reached its peak. We had to walk in threes in order to stay upright. And we had to be prepared to build an igloo not far from the place where the ceremony was to be held. We were all armed with large snow knives and thrust our way with faces bowed close to the ice towards the little village in which the ceremony was to be held. Kingiuna and his partner were holding me under the arms.

' "That is the infant Narsuk crying, and the storm is whistling through his napkins." And now they told me the ancient myth of the giant's son who took vengeance on men, after they had killed his father and his mother, and who rose into the sky and turned into a storm. Today they hoped to discover in the course of the night the cause of the child's anger and try to tame the storm. The wind dragged at us so violently that at times we had to stand still and cling to one another in order not to be blown into the pack-ice that towered up all around us. Violent gusts of wind blowing from the land lashed us as though with whips; only after several minutes were we able to take a few steps forward, until the squall, followed by the shouts of the storm-boy, pinned us down again, almost hurling us down on the ice. I believe that the half kilometre took us a whole hour. How glad we were when we finally caught sight of the warm rays of the blubber lamps within the glistening slabs of ice of the ceremonial hall. We crawled through the long entrance, through a seething mass of dogs which growled and snapped at us, till we reached the hall, where every place was already occupied by men and women.

'The ceremonial house consisted of two igloos joined together. One of the hosts welcomed me heartily and led me to my place. The igloo, which was 13 feet wide and 20 feet long, had such a high ceiling that the builder had had to support it with two beams of driftwood, which made two splendid pillars in the white igloo. There was so much room on the floor that the children of all the neighbours were able to play tag round the pillars during the preparations for the ceremony.

'The introduction to the ceremony consisted of a feast comprising dried salmon, blubber, and frozen, unskinned seal carcasses. The guests hacked at the frozen banquet so that chips of meat flew in all directions. While the warmth of the igloo brought colour into all the faces that had been seared by wind and snow, the guests devoured with great gusto the hunks of meat, which they first blew upon in order not to tear the skin from lips and tongue.

' "Lovers of good food, tough and always ready for a feast," "Eider Duck" whispered to me, his mouth full of frozen blood. And in truth one not only needed a strong stomach for this food, but also strength of mind to make a feast out of a snowstorm. The shaman of the evening was Horqarnaq, a young man with intelligent eyes and swift movements. There was not a trace of falsity in his face; perhaps for this reason it took longer than usual until he went into a trance. He explained to me that he had only a few helping spirits. There was the spirit of his dead father and his helping spirit, a troll of the saga, a giant with claws so long that he could pierce right through a man's body if he merely scratched him a little. And then there was a figure which he himself had made of snow, a figure like a human being, a spirit which came when he called it. A fourth and mystical helping spirit was a red stone named Aupilalangguaq, a curious stone that he had found while hunting reindeer. It was exactly like a head with a neck. When he shot a reindeer close to it, he put a headband made from the reindeer's long neck hairs round the stone. In this way he made his own helping spirit a magician and doubled its power. These helping spirits he was now to conjure up. He began the seance with a modest speech saying he could not do it. All the women of the village stood round him in a circle and encouraged him with cheap chatter. "Of course you can, it's easy for you because you're so strong." But he continually repeated: "It is a difficult thing to speak the truth, it is a difficult thing to conjure up hidden forces."

'For a long time he retained his gravity and his almost provocative assertions of inadequacy, but the women around him did not cease to urge him on, and at length he went slowly into a trance. At the same moment, the men came up too, the circle around him became denser and denser, and everyone shouted encouraging words to him concerning his ability and strength.

'Horqarnaq's eyes grow wild. He opens them wide and seems to be peering into great distances. Every now and then he spins round on his heel, his breathing grows more irregular and he no longer recognizes his fellow villagers. "Who are you?" "Your neighbour," they answer him. "Are you all here?" "Yes, apart from the two who have gone east on a visit."

'But it is as though he does not hear anything that is said to him; he keeps repeating: "Who are you, are you all here?"

'Suddenly he looks wildly towards "Eider Duck" and me and shouts: "Who are those two? I do not know their faces."

' "Men who travel round the world, men whom we like, friends who would like to hear what wisdom you can bring us."

'Again the young man turns in a circle, looks each individual in the eye, stares more and more wildly about him and finally repeats like a weary man who has travelled a long way and now collapses: "I cannot, I cannot!"

'At the same instant we hear a gurgling sound and a helping spirit has come to dwell in his body. An alien power has taken possession of him, he is no longer himself and no longer in control of his words. He dances, jumps, throws himself to the ground among the crowd of spectators and calls upon his father, who has become an evil spirit. His father died only a year ago, and his mother, the widow, who is still mourning the loss of her breadwinner, groans heavily and breathes deeply and tries to calm her wild son. But the rest shout out in confusion that he should go on speaking and repeat the words of the spirit. The young man names several spirits of dead people which he sees here in the igloo among the living. He describes their appearance, old men, old women, whom he has never met, and demands that the others shall say who they are. Perplexity, silence, finally whispered discussion among the women. Hesitantly people come forward and give the name of this or that dead person whom the shaman's description might fit.

' "No, no, no, not him."

'The men stand mute and expectant, while the women cry out in a shrill descant. They are no longer perplexed but only excited. They are on the hunt for the solution of the riddle. Only the widow of the dead man who is supposed to be present sighs in despair and rocks her head to and fro, weeping. Suddenly an old woman, who till now has remained silent on her bench, jumps up and cries out the names of a couple who have only just died, whose graves are still quite fresh.

' "Quanorma! Quanorme!"

' "It is they, it is they!" cries the shaman in a shrill voice, and an inexplicable mood of terror descends upon all the guests, because these two people were moving among them alive only a few days ago. Now they have become evil spirits which call up storm and tempest. Mysterious life has poured out mystic night over all of them. Something inexplicable is happening and bewildering them all.

'Outside the storm is howling, you cannot see your hand in front of your face. And even the dogs, which in the ordinary way are driven out of the igloo with kicks, are allowed to seek warmth and shelter between the legs of the excited people. This is the third day the storm has continued. The people have no meat for tomorrow, nothing to eat, nothing with which to warm themselves, and this threat seems suddenly to come to life. The storm-boy is weeping, the women wailing and the men muttering unintelligible words. The seance has been going on for about an hour, accompanied by shouting and the conjuring up of unknown forces, when something happens that terrifies us, who have never been present at the taming of the Storm God. Horqarnaq jumps forward, seizes good-natured old Kingiuna, who is just intoning a pious song to the Mother of the Sea Creatures, by the throat and shakes him brutally to and fro, to and fro. To begin with, they both utter plaintive guttural noises, but gradually Kingiuna suffocates and can no longer utter a sound. But suddenly a whispering comes from his mouth and that same instant he too is a prey to ecstasy. He offers no more resistance but obeys the sorcerer, who still has hold of his throat, and the two of them stagger this way and that without rhyme or reason. The men of the house have to stand in front of the big blubber lamps to prevent them from being smashed or knocked over, the women hurriedly help the children up on to the benches so that they shall not be injured in the turmoil. This con-tinues for a little while longer, until Horqarnaq has squeezed all life out of his adversary, whom he is now dragging behind him like a lifeless bundle. Only then does he release his grip on his throat, and Kingiuna falls heavily to the floor.

'Thus the storm has been slain "in effigy". The tumult of the air demands a life, and again the shaman takes hold of the lifeless Kingiuna, bites him with all his might in the neck and shakes him to and fro like a dog that has overcome his opponent.

'There is deathly silence in the igloo. Horqarnaq is the only one who continues his wild dance, until in an inexplicable manner calm returns into his eyes. He goes down on his knees before the dead man and begins to knead and stroke his body in order to bring him back to life. Slowly life returns to Kingiuna, the swaying man is set on his feet, but no sooner has he entirely recovered than the dance begins anew.

'The same grip on the throat, the same frenzied racing round the room, the same groaning for breath, until the poor man is thrown down on the snow floor of the igloo like a lifeless bundle again. In this way he is slain three times. Man has to demonstrate his superiority over the storm. But when Kingiuna comes back to life for the third time, it is his turn to go into a trance.

'Horqarnaq collapses on the floor. The old seer straightens up in comical, slightly too corpulent dignity, and yet he dominates us by the wildness of his eyes and the uncanny reddish-blue gleam that has come over his face after the many maltreatments. Everyone feels that there stands a man whom death has just touched, and they involuntarily take a step backwards as, his foot on Horqarnaq's chest, he turns to the audience and with staggering volubility proclaims his visions. In a voice quivering with emotion he shouts through the igloo:

' "The sky is full of naked beings travelling through the air. Naked people, naked men, naked women, travelling about and unleashing storms and blizzards.

' "The spirits of the air are blowing out storm, the spirits of the air are driving the sweeping snow over the earth, the imageless storm-child Narsuk is shattering the lungs of the air with his weeping.

' "Do you hear the child's weeping in the wind? And see, among the naked hordes of the fugitives there is one, one single man, in whom the wind has bored holes. And his body is like a sieve, and the wind soughs through the holes: Tja—tju—u, tju—u—u! Do you hear him? He is the mightiest of all unleashers of wind!

' "But my helping spirit will stop him, will hold them all fast. I see him coming towards me calmly, sure of victory. He will conquer, he will conquer. Tju—tju—u! Do you hear the wind? Pst, pst, pst! Do you see the spirits, the storm, the gale that roars past overhead with the rushing of great birds' wings?"

'At these words Horqarnaq rises from the floor, and the two shamans, whose faces have taken on a transfigured expression after the great storm sermon, sing in simple, hoarse voices to the Mother of the Sea Creatures:

> Mother, great Mother in the depths!
> Take it, take evil away from us.
> Come, come, spirit of the deeps!
> One of your earth-children
> Is calling to you.
> Bite the enemy to death!
> Come, come, spirit of the deeps!

'As soon as the two have finished singing their hymn, all other voices join in like a calling, complaining chorus of afflicted hearts. No one knows what they are calling for, no one is praying for anything, but the ancient song of their forefathers gives their senses power. They have no food for their children when the next day comes. They are asking for calm weather for their hunt, for food for their children.

'And suddenly it is as though the whole of nature has come to life around us. We see the storm riding across the sky in the journeying and the tumult of naked spirits, we see the hordes of fleeing dead sweeping through the billows of the blizzard, and all visions and all sounds are concentrated in the wingbeat of the great bird which Kingiuna has caused us to hear.

'With this the two shamans' battle with the storm concluded. Each of them could fight his way back comforted and reassured to his home igloo and commend himself to sleep, for tomorrow would be fine weather.

'And sure enough, the following day we travelled on in dazzling sunshine over snow blown firm by the wind . . .'[61]

Eskimo drawing. Two restless souls

One of the shaman's main tasks within the context of this type of experience lies in overcoming impeding forces which his soul encounters on its journey. Purely psychic impediments, naturally—a psychological state of paralysis, which he alone can overcome and must overcome for the community.

For the fulfilment of his task a shaman needs dauntless courage and the complete involvement of his whole personality. His activities may place him in imaginary and even in real danger of his life. Lack of courage may cause him to fail in his task. The Salish shaman drowns in the sea if he makes a mistake while crossing over by boat; he is in constant danger of bodily injury at the hands of the hostile powers, the spirits of the underworld. The Altai shaman falls in the rushing torrent that can only be bridged by a 'hair'. Everywhere the shaman is beset by dangers that may bring death on his soul's journey. If he does not emerge victorious from his battle with the primeval mother of the race, the great goddess Sedna, he is flung by her into the abyss, where he meets a miserable end. According to the belief of the Greenlanders the animals and plants of the earth came forth from the body of the goddess Sedna; so that she may be regarded as the 'great mother', the symbol and representative of the unconscious forces which, in their ambivalent function, may be at once deleterious and beneficial.

The shaman is a man specially chosen and therefore more capable than any other member of the tribe of overcoming these difficult tests and obstacles. Hence the essential signs of his being chosen are not of an outward but of an inward nature and analogous to those of the younger brother in the fairy story, who had to be 'of a pure heart' in order to confront danger in safety. Thus the Greenland shaman must have confessed, in order to embark upon his soul journey as a man without sin, and during this 'purification' he must cry out: 'All this because I wish to become seeing.'[62]

Among the Greenlanders, incidentally, not only does the shaman confess, as the intermediary between the gods and men, but immediately after his soul journey a general confession of the community takes place. Among the Altai peoples, too, only the sinless shaman is able to cross the raging water. In other words, it is only through the trials of the preparatory period and the confession that the 'pure man' is able to enter the transcendental world and submerge himself in it.

The shaman's psychological experiences in a trance are always expressed in images from the real world. Such events then live on in human memory as miracles.

The journeys of the shaman into the beyond, his diving down into psychic depths, an experience which we are scarcely capable of repeating, the real result of which, the pacification of the group psyche, the increase in certainty and confidence, remains incomprehensible to us, are generally experienced and reported as a journey to the dead in the underworld, the beyond.

To reach the Land of the Dead the Greenland shaman has to go down to the bottom of the sea, whose realm (mythologically conceived) is separated from the Land of the Dead by a river—the frontier between the Land of the Dead and the world of the living. 'Finally they reached the frontier between the sea and the country beneath the sea, which is formed by a foaming brook; in order to cross it they had to jump over large, sharp-pointed stones that were completely covered by wet seaweed and had such a slippery gleam that no one dared cross . . . With the aid of the spirits, the shaman jumped over these obstacles. The spirits encouraged him and called out to him: "If you do not dare to make this jump, and turn back, you will never reach the Land of the Dead; your journey will always end at these stones." Then the shaman dared to make the jump and to his great astonishment the seaweed proved not to be so slippery at all.'[63] The same author gives an account of steps which the Greenland shaman has to climb in order to enter the World of the Dead. 'The shaman . . . came upon a stairway with three high steps. They were so high that he was only just able to swing himself up from one to the other, and they were slippery with human blood that trickled over them. The shaman climbed the slippery steps with great difficulty and at the continual risk of his life and came to a wide, wide plain, the plain of heaven . . . The way back was without obstacles and he had no bloody steps to overcome.'

Among the Salish Indians of the northwest coast of America the shaman goes through an imaginary voyage by water, in order to recover the lost and stolen soul of a sick man. The voyage across the great sea (River of the Dead), which divides the living from the dead, is made with a crew of ten shamans; the steersman is the spirit of the officiating shaman. The remainder stand during the ceremony in two rows of four, each with a paddle in his hand with which he makes paddling movements. Thus the voyage by boat is made clearly visible to the spectators. After a long voyage they come to the Land of the Dead, the narrows of a river on which the spirits dwell. They fish and hunt, having the same way of life as humans; unlike humans, they walk with crossed legs. By this they may be recognized as spirits. Among primitive peoples the next world is almost always very like this world; the same conditions of life are projected on to the next world.

The first obstacle which the shaman has to overcome in the Land of the Dead is a raging torrent. As the dead are accustomed to do, he lays a tree trunk across the river and crosses it as though by a bridge. While he is overcoming this (imaginary) obstacle, he lays his paddle on the ground and walks carefully along it, balancing carefully so as

17 *Tungus shaman's coat. Siberia*

18 *Rear view of the Tungus shaman's coat*
19 *Right: Iron doll and rudimentary mask from
    coat opposite*

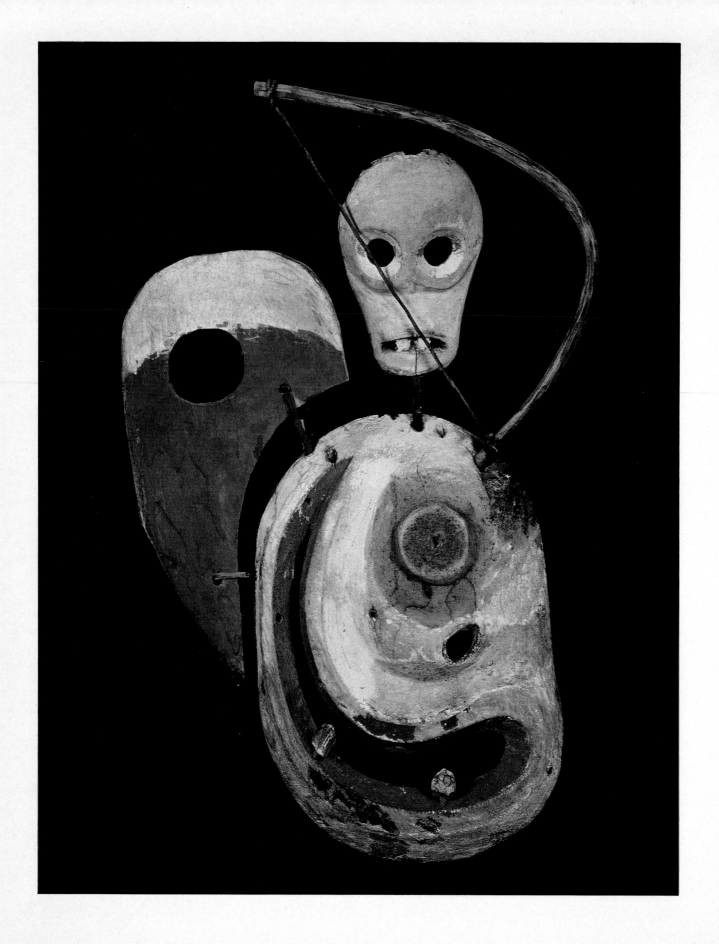

20   *Left: Metal figures representing helping spirits from shaman's coat. Tungus, Siberia (plate 18)*

21   *Two masks from the same coat.*

22 *Painted shaman's rattle from Canadian Indians*
23 *Right: Wooden shaman's mask. Eskimo*

24 Left: Painted shaman's drum. North America
25 Shaman's mask. Eskimo

26 Shaman's mask. Eskimo
27 (opposite) Two metal masks and cloth dolls from
    the Tungus shaman's coat. Siberia
Over the page (28): Painted shaman's mask. Eskimo

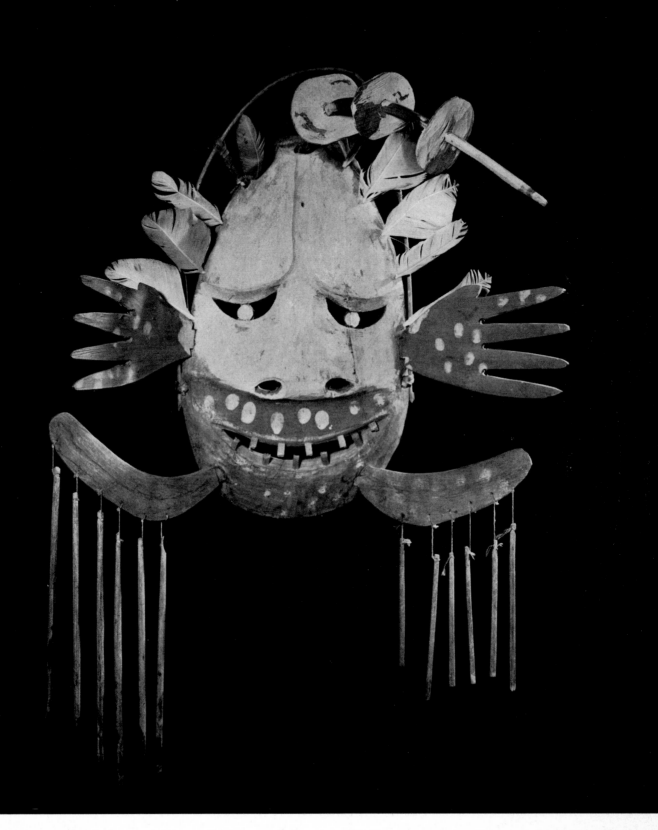

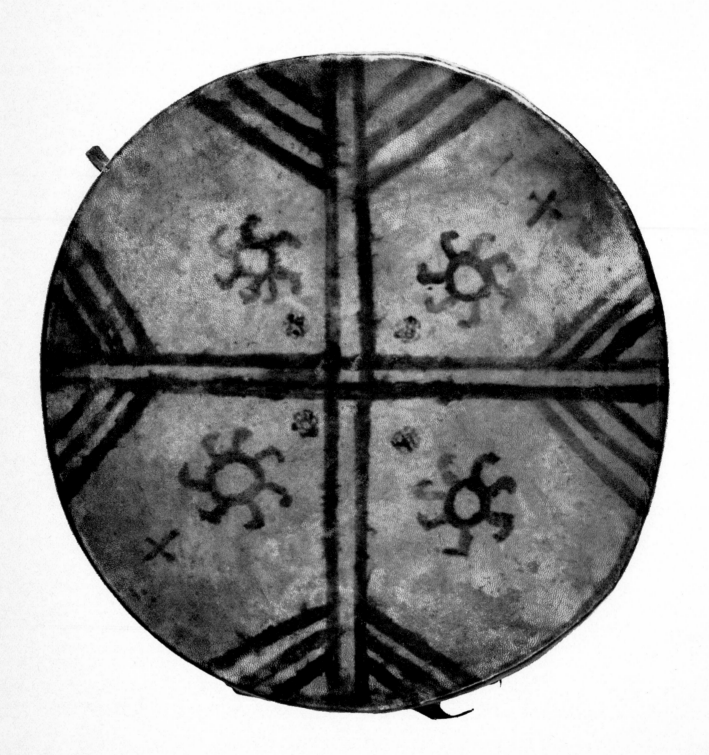

not to fall. The next difficulty is a viscous river that is crossed in a canoe. There follows a struggle with a man who refuses to tell him the way.

As he enters the Land of the Dead he comes into conflict with the spirits, who defend themselves with torches of burning cedarwood. This imaginary battle is portrayed by boys of the tribe, who rush up with torches and throw them at the invaders of the spirit kingdom. According to Indian informants, the participants sometimes suffer serious injury.

Finally the threshold of the Kingdom of the Dead is ceremoniously closed, so that the spirits who have been robbed of the sick man's soul cannot take revenge. When the sick man's spirit has been found the song of this spirit is sung on the return journey. When the sick man hears this music he jumps up and is cured.[64]

We have an account from Siberia on the same subject:

When the evil spirits in the north carry away a person's soul the shaman performs the seance and sets out for their country with various gifts. Formerly old, hump-backed women with putrid bones in their joints set out on the road to the north. They travelled down the Lena in boats and settled on Mount Jokuo.

In addition, the shamans mentioned in particular two old women whom they also drive out of sick people: Tanyakhtaakh Laabyralaan, 'Laabyralaan with a stick', and Toruoskalaakh Soluonnyay-Khotun, 'the Lady Soluonnyay who has a stick'. [The informant is wrong in counting Soluonnyay among the northern spirits. She is usually reckoned one of the nine heavenly virgins, who assist horses and bring madness. G.V.K.]

As offerings to these spirit women nine coarse cakes are cooked and vodka is poured into wooden goblets. A pig and a turkey are made of wood. In addition the skin of a polecat is used, a rope plaited of white and black hair, and finally a two-pronged wooden fork. When these women travelled north they took all these things with them.

Among the spirits there lives a girl with a crooked face who serves as a watchman. When the shaman approaches voices ring out:

'There he goes, the shaman with his heavy load, with valuable presents. Before him he is driving cattle, behind him he is pulling sacrificial animals on a rope . . .'

'Ay, here comes our eldest son (the shaman is their son because his soul was brought up among them). Quick, catch him! . . .'

Then shouts ring out: 'Suu, saa!' (These are cries uttered when herding cattle.) Then the cattle he has brought are driven into a pen.

The shaman begins to speak before them, saying that such and such a human prince has fallen sick and has sent these gifts . . . 'Give me his soul!'

The spirits, satisfied with the gifts he has brought, order the soul to be set free, saying: 'Ay, go and open the door of the prison in which the sick man's soul lies!'

Sometimes the spirits refuse to release the soul. Then the shaman expresses anger and despair . . . He rolls about round the fireplace, turns into a wasp and flies into the cow byre. There lies a bright blue bull. The wasp stings the bull on the nose. The bull snorts and the soul, which lay prisoner in the bull's nostril, falls out. The shaman seizes it at once and flies hurriedly away with it.

The old man, a spirit or a god, leaps after him, throws lumps of clay at him and says:

Drawing of a shaman's ascent to heaven. Altai region

'How annoying! He who yesterday was still being brought up by me, now dares to treat me like this!'[65]

Potanin gives a very fine description of an old Altai shaman's journey:

The *kam* (shaman) directs his way towards the south. He has to cross the Altai Mountains and the red sands of the Chinese deserts. Then he crosses a yellow steppe, such as no magpie can traverse. 'Singing, we shall cross it,' says the *kam* in his song. After the yellow steppe there is a 'pale' one, such as no crow can pass over, and the *kam* in his imaginary passage once more sings a song full of hopeful courage. Then comes the iron mountain of Tamir Shayha, which means 'leans against the sky'. Now the *kam* exhorts his train to be all of one mind, that they may pass this barrier by the united force of their will. He describes the difficulty of surmounting the passes and, in so doing, breathes heavily. On the top he finds the bones of many *kams* who have fallen here and died through failure of power. Again he sings songs of hope, declares he will leap over the mountain, and suits the action to the word. At last he comes towards the opening which leads to the underworld. Here he finds a sea, bridged only by a hair. To show the difficulty of crossing this bridge, the *kam* totters, almost falls, and with difficulty recovers himself. In the depths of the sea he beholds the bodies of many sinful *kams* who have perished there, for only those who are blameless can cross this bridge. On the other side he meets sinners who are receiving punishment suited to their faults; e.g. an eavesdropper is pinned by his ear to a stake. On reaching the dwelling-place of Erlik (the ruler of the Underworld), he is confronted by dogs, who will not let him pass, but at last, being appeased by gifts, they grow milder. Before the beginning of the shamanistic ceremony gifts have been prepared for this emergency. Having successfully passed these warders, the *kam*, as if approaching the *yurta* of Erlik and coming into his presence, bows, brings his drum up to his forehead, and says, 'Mergu! Mergu!' Then he declares whence and why he comes. Suddenly he shouts; this is meant to indicate that Erlik is angry that a mortal should dare to enter his *yurta*. The frightened *kam* leaps backwards towards the door, but gathers fresh courage and again approaches Erlik's throne. After this performance has been gone through three times, Erlik speaks: 'Winged creatures cannot fly hither, beings with bones cannot come: how have you, ill-smelling blackbeetle, made your way to my abode?'

Then the *kam* stoops and with his drum makes certain movements as if dipping up wine. He presents the wine to Erlik; and makes a shuddering movement like that of one who drinks strong wine, to indicate that Erlik has drunk. When he perceives that Erlik's humour is somewhat milder under the influence of his draught he makes him offerings of gifts. The great spirit (Erlik) is moved by the offerings of the *kam*, and promises increase of cattle, declares which mare will foal, and even specifies what marking the young one will have. The *kam* returns in high spirits, not on his horse as he went, but on a goose—a change of steeds which he indicates by moving about the *yurta* on tiptoe, to represent flying.[66]

In analogous accounts from Australia, journeys into the underworld or to the spirits are described as 'flights'.

Such accounts make it clear that these flights are not without victims. For the helping spirits have to be brought a sacrifice consisting of one of the men of the group.

We have here a parallel to the sacrifices which in Siberia have to be made from among the shaman's family when a man is becoming a shaman.

There is no mention of this in Australia, but there are indications that a sacrifice has to be made in connexion with certain rituals.

An essential feature of the Australian shaman lies in the ability of his soul to leave his body while he is dreaming. It is then possible for him to visit far-away regions and on his return—when his body awakens from a deep sleep—to report what he saw and experienced in these distant places. The aborigines speak of this ability of the shaman frequently and in great detail, describing it as a flight which the shaman's soul makes upon a great snake.

When the shaman is 'flying' his body lies in a deep, deathlike sleep, and no one dares to wake him. The experiences of the flight seem to the shaman on waking like a dream. These flight-dreams are of a special kind and distinctly sexual in character. During such a dream the shaman's power 'rises' in his body and causes his penis to become erect.

According to the aborigines, the shaman's soul then rides away on the snake that thus rises. During one of these dreams the shaman's strength leaves his body, but always remains linked to it by a thin thread that comes out of the penis or the navel.

Before the beginning of a dream-flight the dreamer has the feeling that he is climbing a tree, from which he rises up into the air. Often the shaman—in his dream—has to lean a woman against the trunk of this tree and climb over her up the tree. In the air, during the flight, the shaman rides on a snake. Often he copulates with this snake during the flight. Often, too, he believes that he is lying between two snakes which copulate during the flight.

It is said that ordinary mortals can see nothing of these events; they see only the shaman's body lying still. But other shamans can see the experiences the first one is having taking place 'in reality' in the air.

In ancient times, it is said, several shamans used to combine to embark on such a journey. In this way they sent their souls together, riding 'on the strength' of the strongest —as it was called—there to observe certain events and to inform their relations of them. In this way people were enabled to know of occurrences which were often not related by eyewitnesses until years later. But the shamans always proved to have spoken the truth in their accounts.

It also happens that several men simultaneously wish to get in touch with the spirits of the dead or for some other reason to send their souls to a distant country to see what is going on there.

This is done as follows:

The men who wish to go on such a journey sit down one behind the other in a row, looking in the direction in which they believe the spirits to be and in which they wish to send their souls.

The men sit on large dancing-sticks called *birmal*. All the men are linked by a cord of human hair, which they hold in their hands. The first and last man in the row must be a shaman who has already been among the spirits before.

A number of other men sit around those who wish to send away their souls. They

light a fire behind the last man and then sing, under the leadership of a third shaman:
'*Birmal ingalai irir bunga . . .*'

They sing this song slowly and softly without ceasing, until the men sitting in the row go into a trance and their souls break free from their bodies. The song must continue to be sung until, after being away for hours—it has sometimes been asserted that such a sojourn with the spirits may last for days—the men's souls suddenly return, waking them with a start from their trance. It may then often be seen that one of the sticks is covered with blood. This means that someone got in the travellers' way and was injured by the sticks—meaning the spiritual substance of the sticks.

When the men are awake the shaman who led the journey goes to and fro, one to the other, embraces each of them, and they 'rub their bellies together'. According to another report, the shaman touches the penis of each of his travelling companions.[67]

Sacrifices for the shaman

Such flights seem to be very strenuous for the snakes on which the shamans ride. The snakes frequently demand a sacrifice for such journeys. One of the participants has to be killed in order to provide food for the snake. According to accounts given by the aborigines, such journeys of several shamans were often undertaken for the sole purpose of sacrificing one of those taking part.

It is difficult for us to fathom what mental experiences lie behind these reports and what these 'sacrifices to the snake' really involve.

One such sacrifice is described as follows: 'The men sit with a shaman and sing, until they go into a trance. The shaman takes a large snake out of the water; they all sit on it and fly through the air at great speed. They fly so fast that other shamans can see only the quivering tip of the snake's tail. After a time they reach a distant country. There they sit on the ground in a circle round the snake.

'The shaman takes a stone knife and kills one of those present. He cuts him in pieces and gives the flesh to the snake to eat. The other men sit there quietly and watch the snake devouring their comrade. Then they themselves eat of the flesh.

'The shaman cleans the dead man's bones and lays them in a certain order on the ground. He lays out the bones exactly the reverse of the way they ought really to lie. Thus he places the thigh bones on the shoulder blades and the head in the pelvis. The bones are left lying like this.

'The shaman remains behind with them. The other men mount the snake again and return to the place from which they came. But the shaman touches the bones of the sacrifice, strokes them and sings magic songs. Then the bones cover themselves with flesh again; the shaman goes on singing until the slain man lives again. Then he draws from his navel a second snake, the two of them mount it and fly back to the others.

'Then all the men wake from the deep trance in which they have had these experiences. None of the men, apart from the shaman, remembers what happened. Even the man who has been sacrificed knows nothing about it. But then he dreams of a snake, and a few days later he "really" dies.

'It is stressed that such sacrifices to the snake-power have to be made by the shamans from time to time, because otherwise the snake withdraws his strength from the shaman. The aborigines also mention that the shamans always select for these sacrifices enemies of whom they want to rid themselves.'⁶⁸

The idea of the sacrifice is mingled with that of the shaman's ability to kill by magic. It often seems as though the shaman is able to combine the necessary with the practical, that is to say that he offers as a sacrifice a man whom a collective decision of the group has condemned to death.

When the shaman has decided to kill by magic a particular member of his community he gathers the latter's enemies around him. The men go off to a lonely region. Naturally, they announce that they are going hunting, but it is impossible for their true purpose to remain a secret, and the victim, too, will have been able to see from the very choice of the shaman's companions that his life is at stake.

The men go to a bare, desolate plateau in the interior of the country and there sit down in the shade of a tree. On the way they have caught a small lizard. The rough outline of a human figure is cut in the bark of the tree. In front of the tree a small fire is lit. After singing for hours and finally going into a trance, the men throw the lizard into the fire, loudly shouting the victim's name, and then stab it with pointed sticks or bones. These sticks are called *jinbal* or, in pidgin English, 'pointing-sticks'. In Western Australia, in Dampier Land, *jinbal* means 'magical singing'. The figure drawn on the tree is also stabbed with the sticks. In the lonely wastes one often finds trees bearing little drawings of this kind riddled with stab-holes till they look like sieves. When, after singing for hours, the men are certain of the success of their magic rites, they slowly depart in different directions into the wilderness. Many hours later they return and cover the charred and pierced lizard with leaves and twigs. Some informants stress that during such rites one of those present always has to spurt blood from the brachial artery or the penis on to the picture. Others claim to know nothing of any such need.

It is regarded as a certain proof that the magic rite has been successful if, on their return, the men hear just outside the camp a wailing voice, low, but audible far across the wilderness. It makes a sound like 'Gak, gak' and when the men hear it they know that their victim's soul has been burned along with the lizard and is now groaning as it dies. They know that in about four days the victim's physical existence will also have been extinguished.

The aborigines assure inquirers that the victim is never told anything about the intention to kill him. But the bewitched man feels the power unleashed against him in his dreams. Then his soul tells him everything that is happening to it.

Thus, if a man dreams of burning or of seeing a lizard pierced in this way, if he sees 'pointing-sticks' in a dream or feels that he is buried under a stone or imagines that he is treading on the spines which a certain fish carries on its back, he knows on waking that he is bound to die.

The methods employed in this magic rite differ only in detail, not in essence. Thus another method is to coat a stone with wax and pierce the layer of wax with bone sticks or the spines of the aforementioned fish, with the points upwards. Often, too, the figure of a man is first drawn on the stone with charcoal and then the stone is placed with the drawing underneath. It is believed that when the victim's name is called out his soul plunges on to the spikes and is mortally wounded. The song accompanying this procedure goes:

Veila manya manya budu juri jiri.

The aborigines emphasize that it is good and increases the effectiveness of such magic rites if a large number of men are assembled for the purpose. But a powerful shaman can also perform these rites on his own. It is added that these rites can only be carried out at night and must be finished by sunrise.

The aborigines admit that these magical practices have been directed without success against white settlers. But they insist with complete conviction that these spells are always effective against their own race.

A black brought up at a mission station, who could read and write and discuss European politics, once referred to this magic as senseless and ridiculous and said that only very stupid people could possibly believe in it. When I let him see that, contrary to other white men he knew, I did not have a contemptuous attitude to these things, the expression on his face instantaneously changed. The man brought up in the tradition of European civilization and enlightenment threw off the mask and changed before my eyes into a totally different being. In a low, emphatic voice he informed me of the most recent instance in which a man at a station had been killed by 'singing', because he had made himself disliked. The white doctors, 'who know nothing about the singing', had attributed the victim's death to pneumonia.

It is clear that the method of 'singing', which consists essentially in calling the victim's soul by name and then slaying it, can only be employed against people whose 'snake-name' is known. It is, therefore, a method that can only be used against members of the same group or tribe. It is obvious that every aborigine will keep his own snake-name and that of his children as secret as possible.

People whose snake-names are not known are destroyed by the shaman by other means.

In such cases the shaman goes back in a dream to the snake in the depths from which he received his powers. From the depths he takes a demonic kangaroo—the soul substance of a kangaroo—which, however, can also appear to other people in a dream (or also in reality?); he tells this animal spirit the name of the person it is to kill, not the snake-name in this case but the name by which the person is ordinarily known. The shaman can send this animal spirit as far away as he likes. The victim then meets while hunting a kangaroo which always escapes him, mysteriously avoiding his spear but never fleeing far from him, remaining for days in his vicinity. A kangaroo spirit of this kind may be recognized by the fact that from time to time it shakes itself in an uncanny manner. When the victim observes this he knows that he is lost. For the animal is shaking out mortal diseases. The victim falls ill after a short time, his limbs rot and he is beyond saving.

The art of sending out an animal spirit of this kind is called *daba*. The method, the aborigines assure us, stems from the culture heroes and comes originally from the east, from the legendary country of Kalimbi.

When accounts of such matters are being given the informants always add that nowadays there are no longer such powerful shamans; those of today have far less power than those of olden times.

Change in the psychological atmosphere in modern times

In listening to these accounts it is interesting to note how the aborigines—in order to render their reports from the past more graphic—draw comparisons with modern phenomena with which they first became acquainted through the Europeans. Thus, when speaking of the shaman's flying, they always explain that this used to take place exactly like flying in an aeroplane nowadays: the shaman sat on his snake like the white man in his plane.

We can also observe that the old accounts, which are often no longer believed by the younger aborigines, or at least no longer carry their old unquestioned conviction, are becoming credible again through the white man's ability to fly. The influence of civilization has, of course, brought about a complete displacement of actual reality. The great psychic experiences of the past are no longer accessible to the modern aborigine; instead their reality seems to have gained a new lease of life through the 'real' flying of the white man.

An attempt was made to persuade me to believe accounts of the killing and resuscitation of a man—although I did not doubt them in the least, but the aborigine is used to his statements being treated by white men as fantasy and fairy stories—by telling me that white doctors acted in exactly the same way. I was told about an operation which an aborigine had undergone in a hospital and which several others had apparently watched. The man had lain as though dead. The white doctor had killed him; then he opened his abdomen and took out his entrails; he washed them, replaced them in the body and closed the opening. After a long time, the dead man came back to life. He could not remember anything, just as the shaman's victim cannot remember anything that happened to him.

The fact that in northwestern Australia the white doctor generally appears in an aeroplane, since there is no other way of getting to stations deep inside the country, increases the parallels that can be drawn between the shamans of olden times and the white doctors of today.

These parallels strengthen the aborigine's collapsing self-confidence, and from the fact that such miracles are possible in the present and before his eyes he draws the certainty that there must also be some truth in the teachings of his old men. Thus the aborigine living on a station under the influence of the whites finds his way back to the teachings of his race, precisely through his vision of white civilization.

Naturally the profound psychic experiences of his shamans are no less inaccessible and lost to him, for the misunderstanding that leads to such experiences being apparently confirmed or replaced by outer phenomena cannot possibly call back the psychic reality expressed in the stories of the old men.[69]

ART AND SHAMANISM

The influence of shamanism on classical antiquity

Portrayals of shamans from ancient times are relatively rare. Probably many pictures of Franco-Cantabrian art representing animals and especially fighting animals are intended to depict shamans fighting in the shape of animals. The actual anthropomorphic portrayals are easily enumerated.

There is the dancing magician of Laussel, and there are the so-called chamois-man, engraved on a bone, and the man falling in front of a wounded bull at Lascaux. From later epochs we have the representation of men with animal heads and a drum from Lake Ladoga, which are far later than Franco-Cantabrian art, and then the rudimentary depictions on drums in Lapland and Siberia of modern date.

A shadow of Siberian and shamanistic ideas also fell upon the Mediterranean and may be recognized in ancient myths. Thus a basic feature of the Odysseus legend is probably to be traced back to the wandering of the arctic hero known among the Eskimos as Kiviok, who survives countless adventures and finally comes home to his parents. Shamanistic features are also to be found in those parts of the Odysseus legend where Odysseus goes down into the underworld and where the shades are brought back to life by a blood-sacrifice. They also occur in the legend of Orpheus, when the minstrel Orpheus dominates the animals belonging to him—and in the idea of the winged horse Pegasus, the 'poet's steed'. Winged horses or horses with signs of wings are the mount of the shaman, or rather of his soul, when it sets out on a journey to heaven.

Various motifs, which today are only to be found in isolation in one myth, must in earlier times have been far more widespread and important, because they are so frequently portrayed in art. Thus, for example, the theme of a leg twisted or bent backwards occurs only in one myth, but it is a dominant motif in the whole nomadic animal style of Central Asia. In scenes depicting animals fighting, this motif is always used to indicate an animal's death or death struggle. If these scenes of fights are intended to depict fights between shamans, we must assume that the animal portrayed in this manner represents the defeated shaman.

Mistress of the Animals. Painting on a Greek amphora

Shamans' costumes and masks

In all accounts the shaman's psychical experiences during the trance are conceived as real experiences, frequently understood as miracles and spread abroad as such.

Of course, they are no less real because they are 'only' psychic realities. Moreover, the shaman's trance produces a real effect in the psyche of the audience. The latter never remain mere onlookers, but are stirred to the depths by the shamanistic trance. They experience a process of transformation—a catharsis—a purification and ordering of the psyche, an increase in self-confidence and security. All this renders them better able to stand up to the dangers of everyday life.

The shaman's experiences in the trance are consciously and unconsciously transmitted to the others. In order to convey to the others the increase in psychic potency acquired through the trance, the shaman employs a variety of means of artistic expression. Here we find quite simple details: pictorial representations or symbols, colours in the clothing, masks or carefully worked out theatrical performances, dramatized portrayals of a myth and the like. It is not only in connexion with the trance that the shaman engages in artistic creation; he also paints, draws, and composes poetry. A whole series of themes of rock-paintings from the Magdalenian period down to the present exhibit a shamanistic content.

This is not immediately visible—we have to know the world and ideas of shamanism in order to see the shamanistic significance of the rock-paintings.

The poetry, however—the accounts of the shaman's experiences—is immediately recognizable as shamanistic in its lapidary language and its symbolism. The words, the 'texts', are supplemented by a vast number of accessories: robes and masks, the drum as a musical instrument, scenery of branches and so on.

All these effective appurtenances are laden with symbolism for members of the group, every detail points towards the shamanistic myth and ritual that is to be performed, everything heightens the receptiveness of the audience—who are not to remain onlookers, but, if they are not actually to participate, must at least undergo an influence and, through their part in building up the supernatural atmosphere, must contribute to the shaman's trance.

The following paragraphs can give only a general survey of shamanistic art and its elaboration and only one or two selected themes can be pursued in all their variations and geographical distribution. One important work of art that is full of importance is the shaman's dress with all its accessories. Real shaman's costumes continued in use down to modern times only in Siberia. Among the Eskimos, the shaman was distinguished from other members of the tribe merely by details—amulets, belts or headbands; in other regions, rattles, 'magic wands', head-coverings or body-painting mark out the shaman.

The shaman's costume with its accessories constitutes an essential component of the shamanistic seance. Naturally we cannot give a complete description of shamanistic costumes, but can only discuss their typical features in relation to their general symbolic significance. A study of the shamanistic costume provides a direct insight into the whole nature of shamanism that can scarcely be acquired in any other way. In considering the costume we shall distinguish between the headgear—e.g. hats, crowns, masks—and the robes with their multiple embellishments and appendages.

In the first place the shaman's garment, with all its attributes, is an animal disguise. Gloves, shoes, caps and masks also indicate this, and the oldest portrayal of a shaman—that of the 'sorcerer' in the Trois Frères cave—shows a shaman disguised as an animal.

The Eskimos say of the shamans' masks that they are intended to recall a time when there was no difference between men and animals or when beings could take on animal or human form at will.

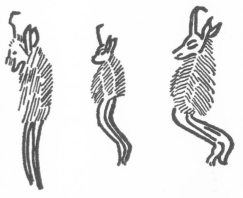

Dancers disguised as chamois. From Teyat, Dordogne (Magdalenian)

The shaman's disguise as an animal is perhaps not so much an attempt to get 'back to the animal' as to depict and absorb into himself the helping spirits that are imagined in animal shape. Often drawings of skeletons, ribs or leg bones are attached to the shaman's clothes. These drawings naturally refer to the so-called skeleton magic and the shaman's development through the process of being 'cut up', that is to say they recall the particular experience of dying and coming back to life that forms part of the shaman's psychic evolution.

These skeletal designs, however, if we look at them correctly, are a resumption or continuation of the so-called X-ray style in the shaman's costume. The X-ray style, which appears at a very early date in rock-paintings and has actually been preserved in the painting of Lapp drums, portrays the internal organs of animals. The style is a reference to the hunting peoples' ceremonies for restoring life to dead animals, based on the belief that the animals they had slain could be resurrected from vital parts, the bones or heart.

Ritual headgear has always played a special role in the ceremonies of primitive peoples, indeed of all peoples. In the first place, it serves the wearer as a protection against injurious influences emitted by hostile powers. In order to counter the demonic attacks that threaten him on his journey through the spirit realm, the shaman wears a head-covering that is terrifying, or at least renders him unrecognizable, and is usually made up of the appropriate animal attributes.

Among certain tribes of Northern Siberia it is the skin of the horn-owl that affords protection against evil spirits. Among many Samoyed tribes (the Karagass and Soyot) there are 'helmets decorated with feathers' of the golden eagle and horn-owl, the head and wings remaining attached. The significance of caps made from the skin of the horn-owl is that the owl pursues the evil spirits and devours them. Hence the shaman who wears the skin of a horn-owl on his head is safe from evil spirits.[70]

Among the Amur peoples of Manchuria the shaman wears during shamanistic rites a wig made of various animal skins, which covers his head like a mane. 'The shaman ties the ends of all these strips together and sews them to the ordinary Manchurian felt cap, to which a few small horns of metal . . . and a large number of bells have been attached. The shamans of the Amur peoples also make their caps of the skins of bears, wolves, raccoons and foxes.'[71]

Probably, however, these animal skins are not intended merely to act as symbols of the helpful animal spirits and to represent the presence of those spirits which assist the shaman in performing his duties. Frequently they also transfer to the shaman their animal qualities, thus, for example, among the Yenissei the antlers as the symbol of the stag bestow the qualities of the swift runner. Nioradze reports that the shamans there often wear a head decoration 'made in the shape of a metal crown and having a stag's antlers on top and a dagger at the side'.

Among the Altai peoples the head-covering is made of a piece of reindeer skin, the front of which is a piece of brightly coloured fabric and is closed with two metal buttons. The Russian ethnologist Potanin mentions hats among these peoples that are decorated with eagle or owl feathers. Further embellishments are cowrie shells and small tassels of fabric attached by leather thongs. The tassels are meant to symbolize snake spirits.[72]

The head-covering does not have for its wearer merely the significance of a protection against malevolent spirits or the acquisition of the desired characteristics of an animal, but is frequently also to be regarded as a distinguishing badge and is bestowed as a sign of rank. Thus among some tribes the head-covering is considered a badge of shamanistic dignity bestowed either by the spirits or by a shaman teacher. An instance of the former is to be found among the Teleut tribes of the Altai Mountains; the hat represents a particular grade of shamanhood. 'Some Teleut shamans make their hats of brown owl's skin. It is not all shamans who have the right to wear the brown owl hat; during the ceremony of *kamlanie* the spirits reveal to their favourites that the time has come when they may prepare this professional dress.'[73]

From these statements it may be seen that among the Teleut the wearing of a hat is not permitted to all shamans but only to certain favoured ones and is considered a distinction.

Among the Buryat, where the shaman undergoes a special initiation ceremony, the candidate, after ritual washing, receives an iron hat shaped like a crown and made of a hoop with two crossed hoops attached to it. At the tip are attached a narrow iron plate and two horns.[74] Nioradze also reports of the Buryat shamans that they receive from the spirits the command to make themselves a hat as a sign of their dignity.

'In order to acquire the full rights of a shaman, the future shaman must see in a dream his guardian spirit *seon* and receive from him the command to make a hat, in order to obtain permission to enter the next world. Thereupon the shaman makes himself a costume, chooses one or two assistants who dry the leaves of a marsh plant in

A masked, dancing shaman. Trois Frères Cave, southern France (Magdalenian)

the smoke for him, invites his fellow tribesmen to drinks and solemnly announces his shamanhood.'[75]

From this report we can see that the shaman's hat is a pre-eminent attribute of an approved shaman, that its precise shape and construction are ordered by the guardian spirit, and that in these cases the hat is regarded as a kind of badge.

The old complete shaman coats of the Yakut, Tungus, Buryat, Yenisei, and Yenisei-Ostyak among others include iron pendants that imitate the ribs, the collarbone, arm and leg bones and the jaw and kneecaps (see illustrations in Holmberg, Harva, Findeisen, Nioradze). Detailed study of the various Siberian shaman's garments have revealed that the majority of the old complete coats were intended as a whole to portray an animal. Birds (owl), cervids (reindeer, roebuck), and bear are the three main types of costume the distribution of which is being used as a basis upon which to reconstruct specific culture areas; an attempt which, in spite of many deviations, seems likely to be successful.[76/77]

Drawing of a reindeer in the X-ray style on a Lapp drum

Holmberg draws the following conclusions from the animal character of the costume. Every original costume aims with all its parts at representing the nature of a particular animal, in connexion with which the iron plates attached to the surface of various parts of the costume stand for the bones of the animal's skeleton. Before the advent of iron, these parts were represented by the natural animal substances (horn and bone). This is also attested by Schirokogorow [78] and L. P. Potapov,[79] who describes the costume of a mighty Tungus shaman as representing a stag, the iron pendants standing for its skeleton and antlers. Schirokogorow expresses the same view on the basis of his field studies. To the headpiece of the costume, representing a stag, iron horns are attached, while the individual appendages of the coat again represent the stag's skeleton. The bird costume of the Tungus of Barguzin and Nercinsk represents a bird—the manifestation of one of the chief shamanistic spirits. It is hung with iron pendants and tassels symbolizing the bird's skeleton and plumage.

Masks are also frequently worn during shamanistic rites. For example, the Buryat used to use large masks of wood, leather, or metal. These were painted and trimmed with beards of animal hair.[80] The Koryat likewise used to possess wooden masks, but these are no longer in existence. The shamans of the Chernev Tartars made masks of the outer bark of the birch and used squirrel tails to reproduce effective eyebrows and hair.[81]

An additional significance of the head-covering is the psychologically important fact that through being thus shrouded the wearer can perceive only to a limited extent external impressions that might otherwise distract him.

The eyeholes, if there are any at all, greatly restrict the mask-wearer's field of vision. He is entirely concentrated upon his inner world of images, so that he waits passively for the coming of the spirits—as is well known, one can best prepare oneself for an inner experience with one's eyes closed. Similarly, the shamans of the Lapps and Samoyeds have the custom of covering their faces with a handkerchief during shamanistic rites.[82] The shamans of the Altai peoples and the Buryat often cover their faces with tassels that dangle from the headgear, while the Samoyeds cover their faces with a cloth.[83] A typical masklike head-covering is illustrated by Nioradze. It is a Soyot shaman

Karagass shamaness's head-dress

wearing a head-covering made of an animal skin and trimmed with feathers, from which a close row of cloth tassels hang down over his face, creating the impression of an animal rather than a human face.

Finally, among the Altai peoples many shamans wear no headgear or mask at all, but paint their faces with soot.[84] Another method of portraying the shaman, the animal spirit or the helping spirit, is represented by the masks of northwestern America. These masks can be opened up, revealing a human face under the animal mask, an artistic technique which admirably demonstrates that several spiritual beings may be combined and imagined in one person.[85]

However, the ideas connected with the masks are more complicated than might at first sight be supposed.

In Siberia, shamanistic masks are comparatively rare. They really only occur among the Tungus and the Mongols. Among the Altaians and Goldi the face is merely smeared with soot. The painting and the mask have a purely defensive character. The shaman would die if he could not conceal his face in the underworld, which he visits on his dream journeys.

Among the Eskimos in Alaska masks are frequent. Here the influence of the masks of northwestern America and Oceania is clearly visible.

Here the mask expresses the dual nature of the being; the animal also has a human double. This dual nature is frequently expressed in North-West Africa by masks that open, and among the Eskimos by double masks; that is to say, one half of the face is human, the other animal.

The mask is intended to recall times past when beings were still able to change their shape. In the present, the shamans are the only ones to whom such transformations are still possible.

Such masks, which express a dual nature, are called *inua*.

Another kind of mask, for which extremely arbitrary and fantastic shapes are chosen, is called *tunghart*. They represent the shaman's helping spirits. They may stand for sicknesses, the elements, places, or combinations of all these phenomena.

Such masks often have smaller amulets or masks attached to them, representing less powerful helping spirits.

The masks are used during trance seances aimed at obtaining good hunting. The helping spirit is begged, or else forced by the shaman, to show him the way to the animals, the soul-places of the animals, or the Mother of the Sea Creatures.

Eskimo masks often have appendages attached representing helping spirits, indeed the whole mask is often nothing but a depiction of the helping spirit.

Very often Eskimo masks are surrounded by small rods or threads, so that they look as though they were attached to the centre of a spider's web or as though the shaman was wearing some kind of 'antennae' round his head.

The meaning of these attachments is not altogether clear, but perhaps the association of ideas with antennae is not to be dismissed out of hand. The strings and rods may represent links with the spirits.

Something similar is to be found in Oceania. In Australia, neighbouring New Guinea, and in various places throughout the South Seas we find in rock-paintings

Drawing of a spirit. From northwest Australia

depictions of the skeleton that are sometimes reduced simply to a centre line with cross-strokes at regular intervals.

Symbolic skeletons in the form of rods with strings stretched across them, so-called *waningis*, are also used in dance ceremonies. These *waningis* extend from North-West to Central Australia. Their significance is by no means unequivocal. But that they are intended to symbolize skeletons is clear from a remark made in north west Australia, where the *waningis* being used during a dance were described as 'bones of the dead'.

E. Worms illustrates very elaborate *waningis* from the Yaoro in north west Australia with the comment that these are representations of the dead.[86]

These *waningis*, generally referred to in the literature as thread crosses and widely distributed, have also frequently been termed 'spirit traps'—doubtless on the basis of fragmentary statements by natives. Again and again it was stated that the spirits of the dead dwelt on these strings and rods. They are not 'traps', however, but abstracted portrayals of dead souls; evidently a form of portrayal that goes very far back and is connected with the belief, which also exists in Australia, for example, that the shaman can journey to the dead in the underworld on a string, a so-called soul-string.

Any further speculation as to whether these ideas have any connexion with the game of cat's cradle, which undoubtedly displays in an early form a fully developed capacity for abstraction and the conception of space, must be left open.

The clothing which the shaman puts on for the exercise of his office is specially chosen and suited only to this purpose. Among the Siberian peoples it consists of a shirtlike overgarment, which in the interior (among the Tungus, Yakut, Yenisei) is made of skins, especially reindeer skins, and on the east coast of sealskin and fish skins. Among some southern Siberian tribes (Buryat, Soyot, Beltir) the coat is made of cloth. The simple shirt form is generally worn over short trousers with high boots. Exceptions to this are the coats of the Tungus and Yenisei, which are cut like a coat running to a point at the back. According to Schirokogorow, this garment as worn by the northern Tungus is a bird or stag costume. When it is used as a bird costume the appropriate head ornament is a bird's head, while the shoes are made to look like bird's claws. Numerous appendages symbolize the bird's wings and feathers.[87] In accordance with the legend, this bird is undoubtedly the eagle, for the first shaman whom the deity sent down to earth to aid suffering humanity was an eagle. When the costume represents the stag, a stag's antlers are worn as head decoration. Here, too, the garment exhibits numerous appendages that are meant to symbolize the swift legs of the stag.[88] In general, all shaman's costumes resemble each other.

In days gone by the making of the garment was accompanied by certain ceremonies. 'Thus among the Yenisei the shaman himself slew a reindeer, liberally sprinkled all the accessories of his garment with the animal's blood and made a coat from the skin.'[89] The blood stands here for the transference of the strength of the animal's spirit. The reindeer's spirit is transferred to the man and so endows the shaman with all its qualities, which he needs in order to fulfil his tasks.

Finally, we must mention certain peoples who do not put on any special costume while shamanizing. Some Tartar tribes and a part of the Teleut wear ordinary clothes while practising their cult.[90]

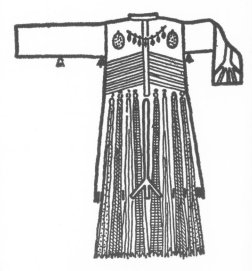

Karagass shaman's coat

An essential component of the shaman's costume are the various attributes that dangle from the coat. Each one is an expression of shamanistic fantasy and has a particular meaning, but nowadays this meaning has faded away, so that the shaman can give no complete information on the subject. Hence great caution is called for in interpreting the largely fragmentary data.

The multifarious appendages are attached either to the shaman's coat itself or to the belt. Some of them are animal and human figures, considered to be the shaman's helping spirits; others are disks of copper or iron, small bells, strips of leather or the skins of small animals, ribbons, rods, etc. Each of these objects has a symbolic significance. 'According to the belief of these people these iron objects and pendants on the shaman's coat have a soul of their own.'[91]

Often individual parts of an animal's body modelled in metal are to be found; they are to be regarded (*pars pro toto*) as symbols of the whole animal. Thus on the Loanga Coast in Africa ivory amulets are worn to bestow upon the wearer the desired characteristics of the elephant (Pechuel-Lösche *et al.*).

In an analogous manner, among the Tungus shamans, as mentioned above, rods represent the legs of a stag or a horse or the wing-bones of a bird and symbolically confer the qualities of each of these animals.[92]

Many garments also bear six-fingered hands or female nipples made of sheet iron. Other thin rods bent at both ends represent fishing-boats.[93] This pendant also has a *pars pro toto* significance: it symbolizes a fish that probably carries the shaman to the underworld.

Human figures are often to be found as appendages, representing the various helping spirits. Thus one of the most important accessories on the Yakut shaman's robe is a rectangular copper plate, the size of a hand, called *ämägyat*, the surface of which is covered with a drawing. According to the description given by natives, this depicts a man 'with feet, hands, head, nose, mouth, eyes and ears'.[94] But *ämägyat* may also be made in the form of a small male figure of iron or copper.[95] Both forms are considered a badge of shamanhood, are attached by an old shaman to the novice's garment during initiation and are withdrawn from him if he gives up his office. '*Ämägyat* is a being quite apart; in most cases it is the soul of a departed shaman; sometimes it is one of the secondary supreme beings.'[96] This spirit inspires the shaman during the exercise of his office and is therefore called the spirit of madness or of ecstasy.[97]

Among the Uriankhai tribes we find small human figures with a miniature drum in their hands. On the same ribbon to which this 'doll' is attached there is also a small animal figure that seems to be modelled on the shaman's sacrificial animal.[98]

Apart from the aforementioned human figures, animal figures are also found as small pendants on the shaman's coat: birds, which probably carry the shaman to the spirit-world, and other creatures that assist him to perform his duties, e.g. divers, swans, eagles, bears. Other pendants symbolize nature spirits, e.g. sun and moon. Mikhailovskii gives a detailed description of the appendages used by the Altai tribes, though unfortunately he says little about their symbolic significance. 'The shaman's dress consists of the skin of a wild goat or reindeer; the outside is almost covered with a multitude of twisted handkerchiefs of various sizes, which represent snakes . . . Some of the handkerchiefs

30 Hinged shaman's mask. North-west America

29 Previous page: Shaman's mask. North-west America

31 *Small wooden mask. Eskimo*

32   Small mask of walrus ivory. Eskimo
33   Right: Shaman's mask. Eskimo

34   *Handle of a shaman's drum of walrus ivory. Eskimo*

35   *Shaman's ritual utensil. North-west America*

36 *Shaman's double mask. North-west America*

37 *Helping spirit in the form of a raven's head. North-west America*

38 Left: Shaman's mask. North-west America
39 A so-called 'soul-catcher', shaman's ritual implement. North-west America

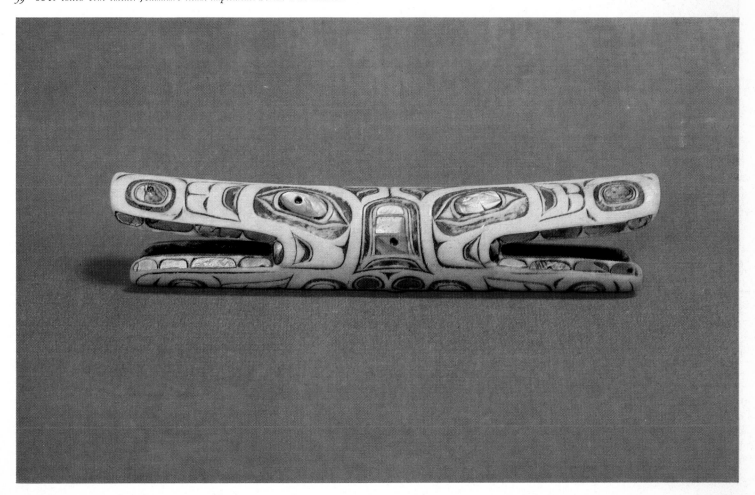

40   *Mask. North-west America*

are not sewed to the dress by the end, but in such a way that the upper end remains free, and looks like the head of a snake. On this are sometimes sewed imitations of eyes; on the thicker rolls, this end is slit, so that the snake's jaws are open . . . It is said that rich *kams* have a thousand and seventy snakes or twisted handkerchiefs.'[99] These snake spirits, too, lend their support to the shamans' power.

Among metal pendants the same author mentions small triangles of iron and adds that iron utensils frighten the spirits. Czaplicka gives as the reason for this that the spirits fear the noise that was made in the smithy while the iron implements were being made. This seems to give an indication as to why the accessories on the shaman's garment were from preference made of iron. Alongside their symbolic significance already referred to, this gives protection against the evil spirits, which are kept at a distance. Other appendages seem in a corresponding manner to attract the good spirits. For example, the bells referred to above appear to be regarded as living beings who call the good spirits with their ringing.

To summarize, let us say that the pendants on the shaman's coat are by no means to be regarded as random fantastic appurtenances, but all represent, or at least symbolize beings drawn from the iconography of shamanism. In many cases they are examples of the phenomenon, well known from the psychology of primitive peoples, of the part of a being standing for the whole.[100]

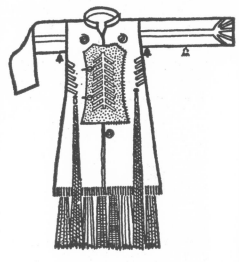

Karagass shaman's coat

Summing up the metal appendages on the shamans' coats, A. Friedrich states:

Knowledge of the real character of the iron bone-imitations is afforded above all by the legends and statements of the Siberian shamans themselves, the legends being the more revealing of the two, for they preserve facts that have already vanished from the minds of those still living. That the shaman was changed into an animal during the seance is attested, among others, by a whole series of Yakut legends (shamans fighting one another in the shape of bulls), and also the ecstatic dances of shamans in which they behave like the animal which their garment and head-dress represent. It is entirely in keeping with this if bone-shaped iron parts of the deerskin costume portray the stag's skeleton. In the atavistic tradition of the hunting era the boundary between animal and man is faintly marked; there is, rather, a close connexion and interpenetration between the two spheres. It will without doubt also have found expression in the conception and portrayal of what is viewed as the being's elemental and vital sub-stratum, the skeleton. But in the shamanistic spirit world the existence of man is by no means exhausted with 'animalization'; this merely contributes, as a powerful root springing from the ancient soil of the hunter's world, to the fulfilment and partial shaping of the shamanistic being. In shamans' accounts of their experiences during the period of preparation and vocation the shamans who have been cut in pieces and resurrected from the bones and flesh of other members of their clan feel entirely themselves in their human nature. And where such importance in preserving life is attributed to the skeleton, a portrayal of the human skeleton on a shaman's garment is easily understood.[101]

Magic rite. Shaman with drum and wolf's mask behind a reindeer. Rock-engraving from Bessov-Noss, Lake Onega, Russia

The shaman's drum

The shaman's most important accessory is the drum—'the shaman's steed'.

In India the drum is still looked upon as a symbol of the Creation. The dancing Shiva is equipped with a drum. In stories of the Zen monks in Japan, the musical note—with its coming into being and its dying-away—is used as a symbol for creation and passing away. Similar views may lie behind the importance attached to the shaman's drum.

Drums are used from Lapland to Siberia. In America among the Eskimos, and farther south among the Indians, the drum is replaced by the rattle. The drums are not merely irreplaceable utensils in enabling the shaman to go into a trance, they are also works of art.

The surfaces of the Lapland and Siberian drums are painted. The painting is figurative and by no means arbitrary; the motifs are interesting and comprehensive portrayals of the tribe's vision of the world.

On Lapland drums, for example, the centre is usually occupied by a lozenge from whose four corners four rays go to the edge, dividing the drum into four fields. The central lozenge represents the sun, the other figures distributed in the four fields—human beings, animals, objects—belong to the shamanistic vision of the world. Some of the figures are gods of the storm, the wind, the underworld; others depict animals, such as the reindeer. The camp or settlement, graves, the underworld are also portrayed.

The gods and the depictions of the underworld are manifestly influenced by Nordic ideas, while Christian themes also find expression on the drums in a simplified form.

At the same time, however, very many ancient beliefs and artistic motifs have also been preserved on the drums. For example, drawings of reindeer on the drums are frequently executed in the X-ray style.

This motif, which nowadays occurs only infrequently and the significance of which is probably no longer understood, links the art of the Lapps with the arctic rupestrian art practised between 6000 and 2000 B.C. in southern Sweden and Norway. This is not meant to imply that at this early period the Lapps were living in southern Scandinavia. It merely indicates that an ancient hunting culture, which flourished in southern Scandinavia in pre-Christian and pre-Teutonic times, has been preserved among the Lapps.

To understand these drawings we must consider the concept of *saivo*.

Manker points out that the drawings which are connected with *saivo* are 'portrayals of the underworld'. But it is clear from the statements quoted by Manker that *saivo* is not the underworld of the dead; the depictions of animals linked with *saivo* involve the concept, widespread all over northern Eurasia, 'of the so-called shadows or souls of the animals hunted'.[102]

The hunter enjoys good hunting when, with the help of a shaman, he has gained possession of the souls of the animals he wishes to hunt.

Manker quotes statements explaining the concept of *saivo*. According to these, every Lapp has certain holy places where his *saivoolmat* gather in large numbers, and these 'family spirits' are at his service on all occasions. In the *saivo* the shamans learned as from their teachers in school, and it was here that the shaman spirit came upon them. Thus in the eighteenth century almost exactly the same concepts lived on among the Lapps as among the Siberian peoples—the shaman's helping spirits which accompany him on journeys, and the images of the shaman's journey to the underworld.

Rock-pictures

Rock-pictures as an art form are a particular manifestation of the hunting culture. Even if other cultures—those of cattle-breeders, nomads or riding peoples—may later have painted rock-pictures, the idea of such pictures goes back exclusively to the hunting epoch of mankind.

Rock-engraving. Animal in X-ray style with 'lifeline'. From Evenhus, Norway

The earliest rock-pictures, and at the same time the finest artistically speaking, are to be found in southern France and northern Spain and date from about 12000 B.C.

It cannot be said that rock-paintings spread all over the world from this first centre and high point, but if rock-paintings are arranged in chronological order, the starting-point must be placed in the so-called Franco-Cantabrian area.

The art of rock-painting in Spain suddenly dies, and its continuation in the so-called East Spanish small-figure rock-pictures is by no means definite. Nor has it yet been established how far the East Spanish rock-pictures, which date from about the sixth millennium B.C., were influenced by early wall-paintings of the Middle East.

From the western Mediterranean rock-paintings extend through the whole of the Sahara and East Africa to South Africa. The temporal sequence of these pictures is by no means clear yet; the only thing that is certain is that fifty years ago rock-pictures in a primitive style were still being painted. The influence of rupestrian art on Negro art, particularly Negro sculpture, has not been elucidated. When we speak of African art we have grown accustomed to thinking only of Negro art, ignoring the rock-paintings or referring to them only marginally, without investigating their influence on Negro art. But this influence must have been considerable and must have operated almost everywhere, even if only as an unacknowledged substratum.

The rupestrian art of the hunters spread northwards over Scandinavia, Siberia, and North America. Traces of rock-paintings made by hunters are also to be found in California and in South America almost down to Tierra del Fuego.

A country especially noteworthy for its hunters' rock-paintings is Australia. The stylistic links of this art with the art of Africa, Spain or Siberia can be demonstrated only incompletely.

The artistic importance of the early rock-paintings, particularly those of Franco-Cantabria, is undisputed; but up to the present art historians have failed to fit this rupestrian art into the general picture of the evolution of art. Wilhelm Worringer has written an essay on this point in which he describes the art of rock-painting as a special phenomenon within art and renounces any attempt to fit it into an historical or logical sequence with the rest of art, because this is impossible. Of course, it is not possible if we seek to place the advance and development of art in a parallel with the advance and development of the material culture of mankind. But this is not necessary. Why should the greatest works of art have come into being when material culture was at a zenith?

On the contrary, there are historical examples to show that this is not the case. The truly primitive, that is to say 'pristine' state of the early hunters caused or enabled them to engage in intensive artistic productivity.

The further intellectual achievement of the early hunting culture, shamanism, is intimately connected with the art, indeed both may be derived from the same basic idea.

Certainly we cannot describe the rock-paintings as a whole as shamanistic art, but certain motifs and whole groups of motifs may be traced back to shamanism or regarded as arising out of a shamanistic attitude of mind, as well, perhaps, as certain styles of rupestrian art.

Unequivocally linked with shamanism are a series of pictures, motifs or styles, which simply portray shamanistic myths or ideas and can be identified as such.

One type of picture springing from shamanism is that in which parts of animals are combined more or less arbitrarily; for instance a stag is given several legs or heads, a panther is decked out with a stag's antlers, parts of these antlers are in turn the heads and hoofs of other animals. Such motifs occur frequently in the metal art of the nomads of Siberia and southern Russia in the first millennium B.C. and are undoubtedly connected with shamanistic ideas.

Battles between shamans, in which the shamans are disguised as animals, also constitute a motif frequently portrayed in early rock-paintings.

Comparable accounts from Siberia of shamans fighting together after being changed into animals are given by Friedrich after Ksenofontov.

'A shaman in our second "Üdügeic Nasleg" named Bodongkos and with the surname Ogusar-Ojun told us that he had come into conflict with the smallpox spirit and had assumed the shape of a bright-blue bull. He said: "I felt that I could be an adversary equal in strength to him. But my wife spoiled things. She opened the door of the *yurta* to see how we were getting on. For this reason he gained the upper hand. My opposition enraged the smallpox spirit and led to seven members of my family dying of smallpox." '[103]

Representations of fights between bulls—knowledge of these myths leads us to suppose that these are actually fights between shamans who have taken on the shape of bulls—are relatively frequent in cave paintings of the Ice Age. The motif even extends as far as North Africa, as is proved by an engraving of two ancient buffalo fighting.

The famous shamanistic painting at Lascaux shows an anthropomorphic figure in front of a wounded aurochs. This, too, is not so much a hunting scene as a shamanistic scene, a fight in which only one of the contestants has assumed the shape of an animal. The combats are, of course, not real fights but conflicts of a psychic nature, battles which the shaman fights within his own mind, in which opposing forces—of what kind we cannot tell—are seen and experienced in the form of animals, particularly bulls.

In view of the hunters' zoomorphic vision of the world, this is not to be wondered at, and it is understandable that such experiences were depicted in rock-paintings, which, however, without a knowledge of the shamanistic stories and the shamans' experiences, we should inevitably take for naturalistic portrayals from the animal kingdom.

If it is possible to explain certain artistic motifs in rock-paintings by studying these

Shamans fighting. Rock-painting from Lascaux (Palaeolithic)

same motifs in other forms of art, and finally to trace them back to shamanism, so a whole stylistic complex, which occurs in rock-paintings distributed over a wide geographical area, can also be linked with shamanism: the so-called X-ray style. In later phases of this style the organs are reduced to a single line running from the mouth to the heart region, known as the 'lifeline'.

The X-ray style

The X-ray style is without doubt an expression of the shamanistic view current among the early hunters that animals could be brought back to life from certain vitally important parts of the body. The mere portrayal of these vitally important parts or of the lifeline brought about the resuscitation or increase of animals. Representations of animals were not merely pictures but contained the animals' vital substance. An increase in their numbers was brought about by touching up the pictures or by performing religious and magic rites in front of them.

The earliest drawings in the X-ray style are to be found among the bone engravings of the Early Magdalenian period in southern France (13000–6000 B.C.); the next comparable works occur in rock-pictures belonging to the so-called arctic art in Norway (6000–2000 B.C.). From here on, the X-ray style in rock-paintings can be followed as far as eastern Siberia, where the pictures date from about the first millennium B.C.

It is a remarkable fact that pictures in the X-ray style do not seem to have spread from southern Africa or northern Spain to eastern Spain or North Africa. These arctic pictures are undoubtedly connected with the Ice Age art of southern France—the path along which this artistic conception may have come to Norway is for the

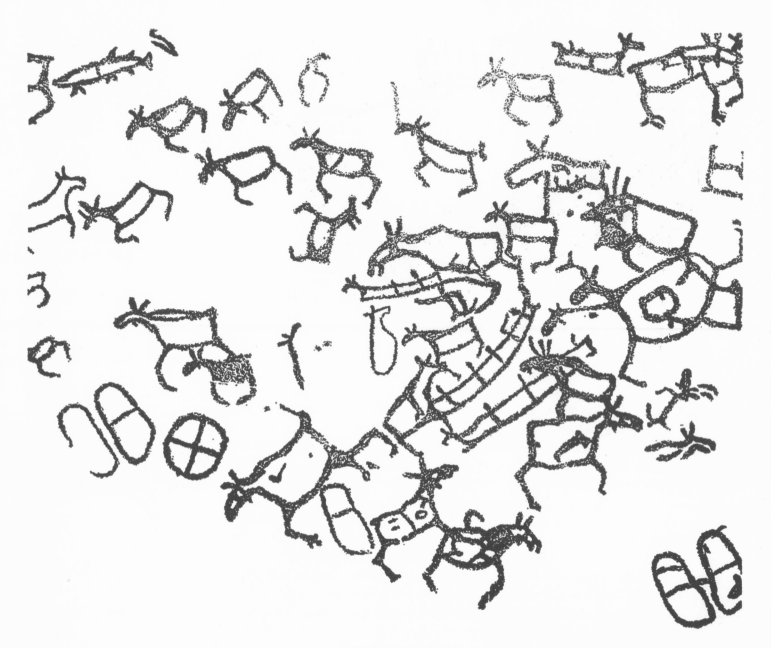

Rock-engraving. Reindeer, some in X-ray style, fish, and symbols

moment unimportant. Bandi and Maringer believe that the style spread first to Russia and from there to Norway. It is in any case certain that the rock-paintings from northern Russia bear a great resemblance to similar paintings in Norway, above all with those of the so-called eastern group. Thus we find almost identical pictures at the two extremes of the area of distribution of arctic art: Norway and the Amur-Ussuri region.

In Norway there are rock-drawings in which depiction of the internal organs is schematized and abstracted to a pattern of rectangles or lozenges. Various stages of this process are found in a single rock-drawing in the eastern group of rock-pictures at Skogervaien, Buskerud.

The process of abstraction may be observed at various stages in Russian rock-drawings, e.g. at Shalabolino. Here the body of a hind looking backwards over its shoulder is divided up by vertical stripes. In one picture the internal drawing takes the form of more or less arbitrarily divided fields, on another of tendril-like arabesques. Here the transformation of the X-ray style into the *à-jour* style has taken place.

From a clear naturalism in the drawing of the animals' internal organs the artists went over to an ornamental stylization of the surface. They no longer remembered the original meaning of the lines inside the outline, but gradually abstracted them; thus the drawing of the intestines became concentric circles or spirals. This abstraction can only be explained by the acceptance of fresh sources of inspiration. This metamorphosis of vision went hand in hand with a change of culture. The X-ray style of the hunting culture was no longer intelligible to the nascent nomadic culture, which reduced it to ornamentation. Naturally, this modification did not take place out of the blue, but was based upon influences and inspiration drawn from the south. Spirals appeared in Russia at least as early as 2500 B.C. with the Tripoli culture, were absorbed by nomadic art and incorporated into the rock-paintings. Later the loose spiral shapes of the civilization of the south were also taken over and then applied to the bodies of sculptured animals—for example in the Ordos bronzes.

These spiral forms take the place of earlier portrayals of wings on the animals' shoulders. A. Friedrich's stories of shamans from Siberia contain numerous references to winged horses, bulls, and even tigers. The references in the stories are fragmentary, but examples in plastic art are very frequent.

Rock-engraving. Cervid with internal drawing. Eastern Siberia

We have here the vestige of an artistic formulation in which Siberian ideas were expressed in the plastic art of the Middle East. The formulations then migrated back to the north. Zoomorphic hybrid creatures, such as winged animals, are frequently represented in the appliqués of Noin-Ula and the tattoo patterns of Pazyryk. According to Siberian accounts, the consecration of winged horses is called for in cases of diseases of the internal organs. There are other references to both artistic forms in Siberian shamans' stories. Thus, for example, the so-called 'inversion of the hindquarters', that is to say the portrayal of animals with their back legs pointing upwards, is connected with stories in which an animal is killed by being so twisted. Here again, references to this theme in the stories are few and far between, but its depiction in visual art is very frequent.

The specific animal style of the nomads of central Asia, which evolved in about 600 B.C., must, of course, be brought into relation with the older animal style of the Scandinavian rock-drawings and also with the X-ray style, and the link between them is the rock-drawing of northern Asia. The animal style is rarely to be seen on rock, almost always in metal—bronze or gold. When this style turned to metal we cannot say, perhaps during the Shang period in China (1523–1028 B.C.), after previously having been worked in an impermanent substance such as wood. Typical of this style is not merely the representation of animals and scenes of animals fighting, but also the depiction of animals compounded of heterogeneous parts and the inorganic agglomeration of parts of animals.

Such fabulous beasts also occur in the early Mesopotamian art, but we must not

Rock-painting. Reindeer in X-ray style with meander-shaped signs. Norway, Romsdal

Animal with 'lifeline', X-ray style. Decoration on pottery, Pueblo Indians

conclude from this that this art came from the Near East. Certain formulations undoubtedly do come from there, but fundamentally the animal style, like the X-ray style of the rock-drawings, must be traced back to the world-view of the early hunters and in particular of shamanism. Both styles are based upon the conviction that a whole animal can be brought back to life from certain vitally important parts, the skeleton, the heart, the lungs, and so on.

The decoration of the animal's body frequently assumes grotesque forms in the later animal style of the nomadic art of central Asia. The body seems to be made up of arbitrary parts—heads, wings, and the like. This style emerged in China during the Shang period (1523–1028 B.C.) and reached its zenith during the Chou period (1027–256 B.C.). From here its influence spread as far as Indonesia, as examples from Borneo show. The simple schematization to an *à-jour* style, for example stripe patterns on the body, need not, of course, always and everywhere be derived from an abstraction of the X-ray style that is no longer understood. In many rock-pictures, especially in Africa, it is clear that the stripes or patches represent the skin of animals with such markings.

Alongside the rock-drawings, the X-ray style has subsisted down to modern times in the decorative art of the Lapps, the Siberian hunting tribes such as the Ostyak, the Eskimos, and the North-West American Indians, and finds its dying echo in the ornamental art of the Pueblo Indians. In North America, among the Ojibway Indians, it was still possible to observe the magic rites for which X-ray pictures were painted. The X-ray style also occurs—even if often indistinctly—in rock-pictures in Kansas, Minnesota, and Virginia. Wilbert even found the last remnants of the X-ray style in South America in drawings which the Waika Indians made for him.[104]

Furthermore, paintings in the X-ray style outside the Eurasian and American zones are known from India, Malaysia, western New Guinea, and a small area of northern Australia—Arnhem Land. Here the X-ray style displays the same tendency to develop towards abstraction as in Siberia. There is no incorporation of spiral ornaments or evolution of an *à-jour* style, however; instead the pictures become increasingly smothered by the locally usual lozenge style. In northern Australia this applies above all to the bark-paintings. The oldest (1884) from Field Island still display a pure X-ray style, but a change towards schematization is exhibited by the bark-paintings produced on Goul-bourn Island during the 'thirties of this century and spreads from there. One can clearly see how in pictures of kangaroos and fishes, say, the internal organs are first portrayed with a certain anatomical fidelity, which is then gradually replaced by a cross-hatching of lozenges, until finally even the shape of the animal falls victim to this process of abstraction.

This development, which it has been possible to observe during the last eighty years, together with the fact that the X-ray style in rock- and bark-paintings is confined in Arnhem Land to a small and precisely defined area, indicate that this style in Australia sprang from outside influences which only made themselves felt on the northern coast and perhaps not very far in the past. As yet, nothing final can be said about the path and the date of this influence. The only certainty is that a tradition of the X-ray style has been preserved right up to the present among the Marind-anim of southern New Guinea and is also visible in the rock-paintings of western New Guinea. A glance at the map shows that rock-paintings in the X-ray style occur from Norway across northern Asia to North America. A second line extends to India across the Malayan Peninsula to western New Guinea and northern Australia. No proof is yet available to support the likely hypothesis that the second line of occurrence is derived from the first. In both areas rock-paintings in the X-ray style clearly belong to the world of ideas of the hunting cultures.

To sum up, it can be established that in Asia as in northern Australia the X-ray style has a tendency, under the influence of other cultural and artistic trends, to be abstracted. In Asia the 'cut-out' or à-jour style comes into being; in Australia a 'lozenge style'. Of importance to further research on rock-paintings is the fact that in the third area of an art of rock-painting produced by hunters—Africa—the X-ray style is unknown.

Not only motifs employed in rock-paintings, but a whole style, can be traced back to shamanism, and there exists in southern Sweden a most illuminating rock-painting belonging to the arctic group (6000–2000 B.C.) in which geometrical figures, in this case acute-angled lozenges and lozenge meanders, occur side by side with animals in the X-ray style—a juxtaposition that is typical and of great significance for our investigations.

Shamanistic ideas as the basis of various styles

This combination of a more or less naturalistic style with one that is entirely geometrical may be observed both in the rock-paintings of the early hunters of the Ice Age, that is to say around 20000 B.C., in the rock-paintings of the arctic group, 6000–2000 B.C., and in Australian rock-paintings, which continue down to the present.

This juxtaposition of styles is probably due to forms having been taken over from other domains of the hunting peoples' art and incorporated in rupestrian art. In Australia we can see the two styles side by side in one rock-painting, and may also observe the continuance of what we may call a ceremonial style in the art connected with dancing, whose geometrical forms are repeated in the rock-paintings.

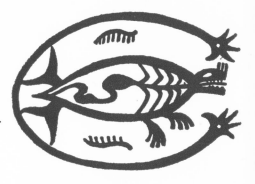

Modern Eskimo drawing. Seal in X-ray style and two-headed snake

Kangaroo in X-ray style. Bark-drawing from Goulbourn Island, northern Australia

In the Australian bark-drawings, where the two styles originally occurred separately, they are today undergoing a process of intermingling. The naturalistic forms of the bark-drawings, which also occur in the rock-paintings, are being increasingly broken down and abstracted by the geometrical style. This latter development is not carried over into the rock-paintings, even those produced at the present day.

In the case of the bark-drawings in the geometrical style, however, the artists always give explanations of the contents of the pictures, which originate from the naturalistic epochs but are no longer recognizable.

Thus in the plastic art of the hunters a naturalistic style is combined with a thoroughly abstract, geometrical style. More rarely we shall find naturalistic representations in a generally abstract picture. Relatively frequently, on the other hand, rock-paintings in a naturalistic manner also contain geometrical details and abstract signs, such as dots, rectangles, meanders, complicated patterns of concentric lozenges, and the like.

In Australia, for example, we may observe that aborigines can give a detailed account of the rock-paintings portraying the mythology of their tribe, but do not know, or pay no attention to, the remains of older rock-paintings in the immediate vicinity of those they are familiar with. Even when these rock-paintings are shown to them and the still quite distinct figures are explained, they are incapable of recognizing such things as human figures, which are perfectly clear to us. It seems as though primitive peoples still firmly anchored in their 'world-view' are totally unable to explain pictures which do not correspond to, or directly depict, this world-view; they seem only to see that which their world-view and their mythology encourage them to see.

In northwestern Australia we find frequent portrayals of a figure known as Wond-shina. This is a culture-hero who is painted with an almost childlike naturalism on the stone under overhanging rocks. For mythological reasons Wondshina has no mouth, but his eyes are depicted as exceptionally large and expressive. In one case the natives proved to be so tied to their preconceived ideas that they asserted of a perfectly normal picture of Wondshina, which had two eyes and no mouth, that this Wondshina had one eye, and standing in front of the rock-painting they began to relate the myth of the one-eyed man. The one-eyed man came from the sea and carried a tree bearing edible fruit upriver, where he lay down to his eternal rest after planting the tree, which has since then grown in the country. The painting showed a two-eyed figure who seemed to be lying on a tree, and was therefore not carrying the tree but being carried by it.

The aborigine guide tried to make clear by winking that the figure had only one eye, asserted that he could only see one eye and could not be persuaded to the contrary.

Obviously, in this rock-painting, the stylistic characteristics of this picture, as fixed by tradition throughout the whole region, had not been brought into harmony with the peculiarities of a local myth. No one was disturbed by this, but the men asserted that they did not see the figure's two eyes, thus, as it were, bringing myth and stylistic formulation into concordance within themselves.

In the same rock-painting, in the midst of the animals and plants and the anthropo-morphic figure—all of which were depicted in the simple naturalism usual in the art of the region—there was an abstract, longish shape divided up by double horizontal lines and filled with coloured dots. This shape might have been taken at first sight for a representation of a snake, the head of which had been worn away by weathering. The aborigines, however, immediately insisted on a different interpretation: this was not a snake, but honey.

Here again the interpretation seemed to be based on mythology, but this time the natives could not give a direct explanation for their interpretation; they explained it by comparisons with other forms which had been included in this picture.

It is well known that in Australia there are ritual objects, either longish pieces of wood or stone disks, which play an important part in the myths. These pieces of wood represent the limbs and the living presence of mythological ancestors. Very often largely abstract anthropomorphic figures may be discerned in their decoration. Frequently these figures are no longer recognizable, but a study of the myths and stylistic comparisons lead us to see in concentric circles or simple geometrical patterns remnants of greatly abstracted human figures.

Carved ivory. Schematized female figure. Mezin, Ukraine

In these ritual objects the spiritual content, the souls, of all animals and plants, of all living beings, and also the souls of celestial phenomena or of certain places on the earth are concentrated. All the phenomena of this world are linked in the myths with certain ancestors. Honey, as an important means of life, is repeatedly connected with a particular mythological figure. It emerged that honey was represented in the rock-painting by a sketch of a ritual wooden object decorated with stripes and dots which stood for a particular culture-hero or mythical ancestor who was linked with honey.

This kind of abstract representation within a naturalistic composition seems exceptionally important. The ornamented ritual wooden implement has become a symbol standing for a particular figure or a particular object and its mythological significance and story. The abstract ornamentation of the ritual implement naturally has itself a long history.

Decorated sacrificial platform. Drawing on a Lapp magic drum

It is impossible to decide whether the abstract form, in which the mythological content is today indicated on the ritual implement, was once portrayed in naturalistic forms, or whether the designs on these wooden objects were always abstract. It is important to note that in rock-paintings abstract shapes appear which have been taken over from other branches of art. The decoration of ritual wooden implements is a different art from rock-painting, so it is conceivable that forms from other branches of art—masks or abstracted dance costumes—were suddenly incorporated in a rock-painting as symbols which, for the time being, are incomprehensible. In any case, the possibility of such elements having been taken over opens up new prospects for the interpretation of rock-paintings.

At the same time it must not be forgotten that this juxtaposition of two different styles in rock-paintings is already very old and occurs in the very earliest rock-paintings produced by hunting peoples. The same phenomenon is evident in the small-scale art of prehistory.

It is assumed that the Aurignacian period in Europe (c. 25000 to 20000 B.C.) came into being when the Gravettians advancing from the east imposed themselves upon the preceding Mousterian culture. From the Aurignacian period we find at the sites of Malta and Buret in Siberia, and above all at Mezin in the Ukraine, elaborate ornamentation consisting of meanders and concentric lozenges on archaic female statuettes. Later,

Schematic representation of human ribs on an Australian wooden ritual implement

Decorated sacrificial platform. Drawing on a Lapp magic drum

Human figure showing ribs. Bark-engraving. Chatham Islands

in the Magdalenian period (15000 to 10000 B.C.), similar ornamental forms occur on utensils.

Can we assume that this juxtaposition of two different styles can be explained, so to speak, historically even at such early times, or must we conclude that the union of two contrary styles in one work of art corresponds, or might correspond, to an artistic necessity that finds expression at all epochs?

At any rate much light may be thrown upon the significance of abstract, geometrical forms in rock-paintings in the naturalistic style by a comparison with similar compositions of a later date and an historical examination of their genesis.

In rock-paintings of the Ice Age, for example at Lascaux, we find representations of wild cattle side by side with rectangles filled with several cross-stripes—abstract shapes frequently described as 'traps'.

Naturally we cannot dismiss the possibility that these shapes do represent traps, but it is unlikely that they are traps in our sense of the word. Probably they are symbols intended to bring about the capture or slaying of animals not so much on the physical, as on the psychical plane. And on the drums of the Lapps rectangular or lozenge-shaped forms occur that can be compared to the 'traps' in the Ice Age pictures.

From comparisons between such motifs, and also from a study of certain sixteenth-century woodcuts, Manker believes, not without reason, that the rectangular, sub-divided shapes are intended to represent sacrificial platforms. These sacrificial platforms played an important part in the religion of the Lapps; they were often decorated with branches, and rudimentary branches are very frequently to be found on the rectangles and squares on the drums.

One possible interpretation of the rectangular shapes from the Ice Age is that, like the comparable motifs on the Lapp drums, they represented sacrificial platforms.

Another interpretation might be given by comparing them with similar shapes in later rock-paintings, those of Australia for example.

Australian rock-paintings do indeed contain similar shapes—subdivided rectangles which later turn into lozenges or vertical strokes subdivided horizontally, which may look like abstractions of trees.

Comparison, above all, with drawings on shamans' costumes make it appear likely that these motifs are the reduction and abstraction of drawings of the ribs. This motif occurs quite frequently in early Chinese ceramics, as a tattoo pattern in the Marquesas and as a dendroglyph on the Chatham Islands to the east of New Zealand.

In Australia the motif is found on ritual wooden implements, especially in a negative shape: the treelike form is achieved by two parallel rows of rectangles arranged so that it is the spaces between the rectangles which depict the tree.

The treelike motif also crops up as a dance implement, that is to say as a piece of theatrical art. This implement is expressly described as the 'bones of the dead'. The dances in question are known as spirit dances, because they are believed to have been taught to the shaman by the spirits of the ancestors.

Here, then, we have a clear statement that in Australia the treelike motif represents a skeleton, which is also manifest from comparisons with forms of this motif occurring in neighbouring regions, where they have not yet been entirely abstracted.

On the other hand, the dance implement in northwestern Australia, and the fact that these are spirit dances, clearly link this artistic motif with shamanism and may also link it with the so-called skeleton magic as practised, especially, by northern Eurasian shamanism. The gridlike geometrical signs in the rock-paintings of the Ice Age are, therefore, probably abstracted representations of skeletons. Their significance lies in the belief in the resurrection of a living creature out of its skeleton. This sign was placed next to the naturalistic pictures of animals in order to encourage or ensure the continued existence, the multiplication or the resurrection of the animals depicted. They are also traps in so far as a sign which guarantees the continued existence or resurrection of animals is also a guarantee of their capture and killing. The figure below shows a schematic portrayal of the so-called thread-cross from Australia. Parallel lozenges run round the intersection of the cross and are centred upon it, while their corners lie upon its cross-beams.

Human figure showing ribs. Tattoo pattern. From the Marquesas

Human figure showing ribs. Pottery decoration. China, Yang-shao (2200–1700 B.C.)

Shamanism and the primeval forms of the theatre

One very important means by which the shaman influences his fellows is his ability as an actor, his use of the theatre and drama. His histrionic achievement lies in his almost complete identification with the 'images' in and through the trance. The myths of primitive peoples are always thought of in dramatic terms.

In the examples we have given of exceptional mental states and of soul-journeys we frequently encounter the phenomenon that the ecstatic shaman takes into his body the spirit of an animal, by which he is possessed. Then the spirit speaks through him as a medium in its spirit language. Psychologically speaking, the whole structure of the personality is thereby altered. The original individuality is suppressed; the imaginative capacity becomes identified with the new spirit individually. Then the conscious ego is extinguished; the spirits, the representatives of the super-ego, are incorporated into the personality and identified with the shaman. Thus the link with the spirit world, the 'collective soul', is established.

When the animal spirit has entered into the shaman he has to behave outwardly in conformity with the animal in question: he howls like a wolf, barks like a fox, whistles like a jack-snipe, snorts like a walrus or bellows like a bull. 'I am the magic bull,' says the beautiful song of the Yakut shaman. If the shaman also wears a mask in the shape of the animal the identity of shaman and animal is almost complete. Naturally the shaman's dramatically manifested absorption in the collective soul is not limited to the case of the animal spirits. Many processes during the soul-journey, in particular obstacles on the way, are represented dramatically; in addition, however, the shaman also acts his own person and his behaviour on the journey. His experiences during the shamanistic seance are often represented by the shaman with magnificent artistry; above all, descriptions of these experiences constitute the poetry of these peoples. Thus in the account of the Salish Indians the journey to the underworld in a boat is made graphically visible to the onlookers by a crew of ten shamans in rows of four carrying out paddling movements in front of the community, while the chief shaman plays the part of the steersman. When later in his journey the chief shaman has to cross

Schematic representation of a so-called thread-cross from Australia

137

an imaginary river he indicates this by carefully balancing his way across his paddle which he has laid on the ground. Spirits that fall upon him during his journey are played by boys carrying torches.

Accounts of the Altai shamans relate that the feelings of the journeying shaman are dramatized. He sings songs to keep up his courage, breathes deeply and heavily when the path becomes difficult and almost falls while crossing a bridge consisting of one hair. All these occurrences are graphically mimed.

The shaman's soul-journey is a mimed repetition of a myth; that is to say it repeats the memory of the travels and adventures of a shamanistic tribal hero of ancient times— a memory that is preserved in tribal tradition, ever-renewed, changing and in this sense 'living'—in whose figure many historical personages are fused into one. Among Europeans only a small residue of such reality-experiences is still extant—in our fairy tales and myths. These were originally experienced as reality and carried out as actions by our forefathers, in a similar manner as, for example, the dramatic rites of death and rebirth in the Egyptian cult of Osiris. In those days, as even now among the primitive peoples, myths were not merely told, as among ourselves, but relived in action, mimed and acted. Hence among primitive peoples myths have all the force of something actually lived and experienced by all those taking part.

In our case, too, myths take place in the distant past; but generally they no longer have such intensity of experience that a need for dramatization is felt. Only in children can we sometimes still observe the 'compulsion to dramatize' that is inherent in the world of images of the fairy tales and myths; they spontaneously 'play' the visual content of the stories, and, vice versa, we may still see in children's games today remnants of myths that were originally acted. Thus hopscotch and certain circle games are relics of ancient initiation myths.

What is looked upon by us as a myth, and has paled into the insignificance of a mere story, is preserved and passed on among primitive peoples as a present reality in the form of a 'dramatization'.

The transposition of trance experiences into artistic form is particularly clearly expressed in the accounts from Australia. Here there is no form of artistic expression that is not manifestly regarded as conveyed to living men by the shaman from the spirits of dead ancestors.

The shaman can go down to the underworld, the country of the dead, and enter into relations with the spirits of the dead and in particular his own dead ancestors, in order to become artistically productive. On this point the Australian aborigines say:

If a shaman speaks with the spirits of the dead, this takes place by his soul leaving him while he is asleep and wandering about the country. At sunset the shaman's soul meets somewhere the shadow of a dead ancestor. The shadow asks the soul whether it shall go with it. The shaman's soul answers yes. The shadow of the dead ancestor then becomes his helping spirit. Then they go on together, either at once into the kingdom of the dead or to a place in this world at which the spirits of the dead have gathered.

The shaman's meeting with the spirits of the dead proceeds according to a ritual that has been exactly described. First the shaman covers his eyes with a leafy branch, in order not to see too many dead all at once, and sits down modestly among those present.

The spirits begin to sing and dance. The shaman must not take away the branch from in front of his eyes and watch the dances until the helping spirit that has brought him there tells him to. When the dance is over the spirits release the shaman's soul and his helping spirit brings it back to his body. When the shaman wakes his experiences with the spirits seem to him like a dream. From now on he thinks of nothing but the dances which he has seen and his soul keeps on going back to the spirits to learn more and more about the dances. His wife may then notice that his soul leaves his body every night, and she will say: Why do you always leave me?

But the shaman will tell her that he goes to the spirits to learn dances. Then he will first explain the dances to his wife and sing them to her, and after that he will teach them to everyone else. That is how the magnificent pantomimic dances of the aborigines come into being.

But it also happens that a shaman loses the gift of frequenting the underworld. He suddenly becomes incapable of making contact with the spirits and his poetic gift for creating songs and dances vanishes.

In such cases all the men gather together to re-establish the broken link with the dead forefathers.

The shaman is laid on the ground. All the men sit in a circle around him. They begin to sing and as they sing they slowly rub the shaman's body. The men sing for hours on end on a regularly rising and falling note:

Mmmmm nnnnnn mmmmmm nnnnn

(This is a humming such as occurs in many Russian folk songs.)

The shaman gradually goes into a trance; finally his soul leaves his body and, so the accounts say, roams about looking for the spirit of a dead ancestor. After long wandering it will finally come upon such a spirit.

The dead ancestors themselves send out one of their number to look for the shaman. They themselves have painfully missed the shaman's visits and the contact with their living descendants and wish to re-establish relations with the living.

The shaman tells the spirit of the dead that he no longer knows the way to the underworld and cannot 'find' any more songs. The spirit of the dead—frequently it will be the spirit of his father or grandfather—promises to help him and to come for him in a few days.

After a time—it is perhaps one evening when the people are sitting quietly and talking—the shaman suddenly hears a distant call. It is his helping spirit calling him. He goes off by himself and converses for a while with the spirit.

But a few days later his soul leaves his body. His body lies quietly sleeping. But under the leadership of the helping spirit many spirits now come up from the under-world and take possession of the shaman's spirit, which they want to see among them again. They tear the soul to pieces and each spirit carries a piece into the underworld. There, deep under the earth, they put the shaman's soul together again.

They show him the dances again and sing songs to him.[105]

Here we have an authentic account of the nature of artistic creativity. It would be impossible to imagine a more vivid one. The symbolism of the language is immediately intelligible. In connexion with modern polemics concerning tradition in art it is especially interesting to note that for these primitives the connexion of an artist's creative potency with tradition, with the ancestors—or those levels of the psyche that carry tradition or 'memory'—is beyond question. If the link breaks and the poet loses his ability it has to be sought for again, and can be found.

The shaman's experiences give him special abilities which afford him his social status. Not simply the experiences, of course, but their artistic transposition into dramatic action. The shaman is not merely the 'sorcerer' who influences fortune in the chase, but also the poet and artist of his group. It is he who moulds the spiritual world of his group into impressive images, and who gives ever-renewed shape and fresh life to the images that live in his group's imagination—the myths, the religious superstitions. To accomplish this he puts himself in a trance and lets his community take part in this trance. The trance is, so to speak, the plane of communication—or communication is achieved through the trance. The religious or artistic rapture, essential to communication of the images, is impossible or difficult to achieve in a state of normal waking consciousness. In the trance the shaman is helped by the group's labile psychic equilibrium, its particular psychic structure, the so-called dreamlike atmosphere.

The shaman is able to influence the psyche of his group, to give it fresh life, to render it creative and restore its healthy, productive equilibrium more effectively than any modern psychotherapist, artist or man of the theatre, and also more effectively than any celebrant priest.

The development and working conditions of these people are vividly clear from the intentionally generalized accounts given here—although they are not entirely comprehensible to us.

Although we can 'understand' from without the psychic processes leading to a man becoming a shaman, we cannot experience them ourselves—which would be the only way of gaining true understanding.

Nevertheless we can clearly see the particular form taken by this first 'spiritual' man from the primordial epoch of humanity, and the nature of this combination of artistic, psychotherapeutic, magical and histrionic abilities; thereby we gain an insight into the early mental life of mankind, which reveals an astonishing complexity, a complicated psychic structure so modern in appearance that we are reluctant to credit so-called primitives with such minds.

It will be worthwhile to look once more at the artistic achievements of the shamans.

41 *Lapp painted shaman's drum. Sweden*

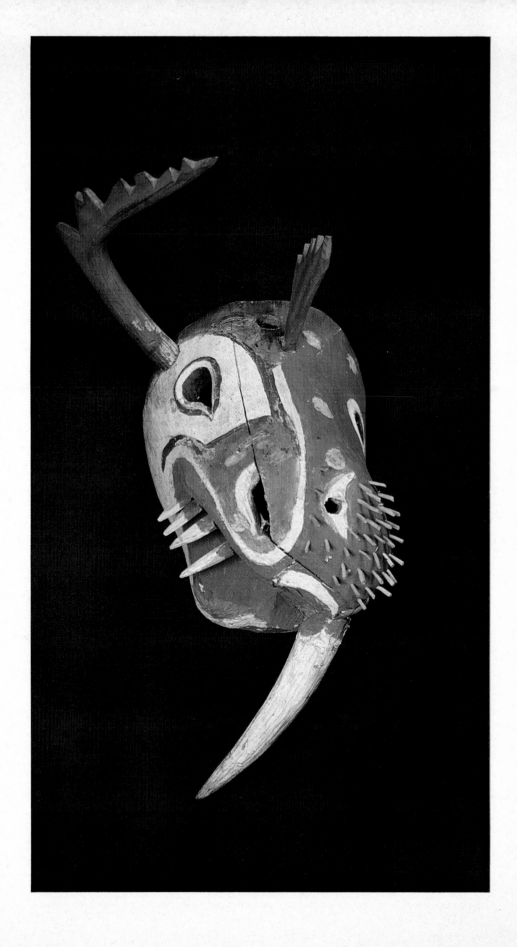

42 Shaman's mask. Eskimo
43 Right: Shaman's mask. North-west America
44 Over the page: Shaman's mask. Eskimo

THE SHAMAN AS THE ARTISTICALLY CREATIVE MAN

Attempt at a definition

In Australia it is above all theatrical performances and poetry that are derived from the trance experiences of the shaman. The shaman visits the 'spirits' of the ancestors in the 'underworld' and receives songs from them. Naturally these songs always remain within the framework of tradition, and the 'images' are those which have always been embodied in theatrical performances.

It is, then, a kind of recollection, but a productive one: the myths and ideas handed down from previous generations are given new and individual shape by the shaman. It has, however, never been suggested that the rock‐paintings or their modern successors, the bark‐paintings, are also derived from the trance experiences of a shaman artist. Are we to conclude that visual art belongs to a different domain?

In the first place the genesis of the rock‐paintings lies so far back in the past that they can no longer be linked with those living today or their immediate forebears. When asked, the aborigines say that the rock‐pictures were not painted by anyone: they are the imprint of deified forebears who lay down to die at a particular spot and left their 'imprint' behind them. It is of no consequence that this imprint appears not on hori‐ zontal but almost always on vertical surfaces.

At the present time no more rock‐pictures are painted—they are merely painted over, 'renovated'.

Since the rock‐paintings contain the soul‐force of the beings which they represent, the current elder of a totemic group 'related' to the rock‐paintings goes to the place shortly before the rainy season and paints over them. It is said that for this purpose he must be alone and undisturbed. It is a fact that white men have again and again come across renovated rock‐paintings and have then found out who painted over them, but no white man has ever seen an aborigine engaged in this activity.

Although the pictures are unquestionably not painted in a state of trance, the painter is nevertheless in a condition resembling that of trance which the natives describe by the European word 'dream'. The word dream is used for lack of any suitable European word known to the aborigines that could express a state other than that of everyday consciousness.

The Australian aborigines describe the time of Creation as the dream time. The first beings dreamed the animals and plants; they painted the dream images on the rocks, filled them with soul-force, and from the rock-paintings the souls of the beings represented spread over the world in a physical shape.

The dream represents the creative condition. Certain people—the shamans—are able to put themselves in this creative state and in it to perform acts that are impossible to ordinary mortals.

The happenings in this dream world are today often misunderstood by the more or less civilized aborigines. They look for psychic realities and experiences in actual reality; they expect miracles. In fact, the 'dream state' is a psychic state which does not correspond to full consciousness and in which man has a different relationship to reality, and above all finds another form of remembering. Events of the real environment are transformed in memory, mingled with dream experiences, and the remembered truth is different from the historically ascertainable truth.

According to the aborigines, in the dream state man has a share in the creativity of nature, and if he were to be creatively active in this state he would really, as the painter Baumeister expressed it, 'not create after nature, but like nature'. Thus we must suppose that the rock-paintings, and probably not only those of Australia but all the rock-paintings of the early hunting epochs of the world, were not produced in a state of ecstasy or trance, but are the expression of this dreamlike atmosphere still to be observed in Australia.

Looked at from this point of view, the assertion that the artists of the Ice Age were eidetics gains increased probability. The transposition of impression into expression takes place by a different, one might perhaps say a shorter, route than with an artist who works in a state of complete consciousness.

It is very possible that a certain elegance of movement, and a corresponding naturalism, are to be interpreted in this light, although they cannot be explained in detail.

The ideas of the early hunting cultures, as expressed in the rock-paintings, naturally circle round the animal, and the art of hunters is almost exclusively zoomorphic. A whole series of motifs in the ancient rock-paintings are purely shamanistic, and we must link the genesis of art as such with the genesis of the shamanistic outlook.

Shamanism in the true sense is a concentration and intensification of the views of the early hunting cultures, and not all the art of these epochs can be described as shamanistic. Certain motifs or groups of motifs, however, can be linked with shamanism in the narrower sense—above all, the X-ray style. This style, as we have seen, extends from the Magdalenian culture of southern France through northern Europe, northern Asia and North America to Middle America and even Australia. Curiously enough, it is not found in Africa.

Remains of this style are to be found down to modern times on the drums of the Lapps. From the ideas of the Lapps concerning an 'underworld in which the souls of animals live' we can understand the X-ray style as the portrayal of the concept—

world-wide among hunting peoples—that a picture showing the vital parts contains the animal's life-force.

Animals portrayed in the X-ray style are neither living nor dead animals, but spirit animals; that is to say, the form and spiritual content of animals, the soul from which the real animals are for ever reborn.

Such concepts, which are very ancient and were elaborated by the early hunters, occur at the beginning of art. The separation which the early hunter made between soul and matter led to artistic representation. The spiritual content of shamanism, which is an attempt to make capital of the recognized or desired separation between body and soul, is thus to be regarded as responsible for the beginnings of art.

Shamanism came into being at a time when man could not help feeling inferior in relation to his environment. He began to carry on the struggle for existence by spiritual means and came to attach special importance to the state of his soul as a condition for survival. A multitude of concepts and rules of behaviour were worked out and systematized with this end in view.

Shamanizing consists essentially in rendering the mythological images of the group tradition lively and productive, in employing them to strengthen the collective soul by depicting them and making them conscious. Thus the shaman's activity is to an important extent an artistic one: miming, acting, singing, dancing, and painting.

Shamanizing is always done in a trancelike state, the trance frequently being artificially induced. It seems that in a state which is not that of full consciousness the images of a group's mythological tradition are experienced by the shaman with particular intensity and, above all, can be transmitted to the group. The shaman's power over his group may be of varying degrees, but it may be so strong that an increase in the shaman's psychic potency is or has to be counterbalanced by a weakening of potency in other members of the group. This may go so far that many reports speak of various members of the group having to die when an important shaman is being formed.

The psychological laws at work in shamanism remain closed to modern man; they can only be reported in the language of the various informants. Nevertheless, if we consider the similar characteristics of shamanism as they appear over wide areas of the earth, the development of the shamanistic personality, its activity, its effect on the group and its importance to human artistic expression, we shall be able to give quite a full answer to the question of what, in the last analysis, shamanism is.

Shamanism is a concentration of concepts and psychic techniques which, in the course of time, have been worked out by a particular group of hunting peoples and have spread over every continent with the exception of Africa.

At a time when man inevitably felt inferior to his environment he sought to assert himself and influence his environment by increasing his psychic force. In the course of his development this attempt and this activity were transferred to particular people. The personal development of the shaman in this connexion is described in extraordinarily similar terms over wide areas.

Almost always the man chosen to become a shaman is sickly and weak. In many cases, especially in Siberia, he cannot escape from shamanhood, even if he would like to. It is not easy to see why a sick man in particular should be called to shamanhood.

A process of self-healing, often regarded as inescapable, a purely psychic process portrayed in impressive images of dying and being cut in pieces, leads him to overcome the illness and finally to gain power over the spirits of disease. Rationalistically it is often added that the shaman had to let the spirits of disease eat of his limbs and that he has power only over those spirits which partook of this cannibalistic meal.

Without artistic creation in some form or other there is no shaman. The question of whether artistic creation under primitive conditions always arises out of such a psychic process must remain unanswered here. In any case, however, it is by giving shape and form to the traditional ideas and images that the shaman overcomes his original condition of psychic weakness, a mental illness, and attains his function.

The increase in psychic power which he acquires in the course of his development is described in all accounts by the concept of the 'helping spirits'. Helping spirits—generally visualized in the shape of animals—are at his beck and call.

Many investigators who have concerned themselves with shamanism have avoided the question of how much reality is attached to these spirits.

It is, however, perfectly clear and, if we bear in mind the particular conditions of the trance or dreamlike atmosphere, entirely understandable, that these spirits have only an inner, a psychic reality, that they are simply images or symbols of a transformation of the future shaman's psychic structure. This does not mean that the helping spirits have less reality—merely that it is not a reality of the external, material world. By means of his 'helping spirits' the shaman influences the people of his group, and this influence is always exercised in a state of trance. The techniques of trance and ecstasy are thus undoubtedly essential characteristics of shamanism.

The result of shamanistic seances is a strengthening of the group psyche, an increase in security and self-confidence. It seems that the transmission of psychic force from the one, the shaman, to the others is best carried out in a state of trance, that is to say in a state in which the waking consciousness is more or less eliminated or reduced. The psychic forces may be disturbed by criticism or fear, and such thoughts or feelings must be silenced at the moment of transmission.

Thus shamanism is above all a method, a psychic technique, with which, in a particular cultural situation, especially in a certain 'dreamlike atmosphere' still achieved today in Australia, psychic images and energies, that is to say traditional ideas or myths of a particular group, can be re-experienced, ordered, intensified, given artistic shape, and communicated by means of the trance of an individual specially prepared for this activity. The result of this activity is a strengthening of the collective psyche. It is a process of bringing order through artistic form to the world of ideas, which has become chaotic through debilitating influences or conditions. The world of ideas, the vision of the world, have to be activated and reshaped.

Modern psychology is an essential point of departure for an understanding of this process. Ethnological methods, such as the comparative history of cultures, can lead to a clarification of the basic features of shamanism, but not to a complete understanding of it.

In the course of time shamanism, and above all Siberian shamanism—through contact with the civilizations of South and East Asia, with Tibet, with Buddhism, with Persia—took over many features which were at first regarded as shamanistic, but which, in fact, are not part of shamanism; that is to say, a shamanism without these features is perfectly conceivable. As the rock-paintings show, shamanism already existed in the Magdalenian period, between 15000 and 10000 B.C., and at this time it was obviously without the later accretions acquired from the highly developed civilizations.

The roots of shamanism, however, go back to the so-called Alpine Palaeolithic, 30000 to 50000 years ago. At the same time, ideas derived from shamanism have naturally exercised a powerful influence on the myths, philosophies, and religions of later cultures, including the high civilizations. Shamanistic influences may be observed in the religious systems of the Near East, in Islam, above all in North Africa, and in the religions of India. The Tibetan form of Buddhism is permeated with shamanistic relics, which are particularly in evidence in the Bon religion.

In art, too, shamanistic features are widespread. Not every animal style, every portrayal of animals in rock-paintings or other domains of art, must necessarily be traced back to shamanism; but there is a series of motifs which is clearly of shamanistic origin. Thus the central Asian animal style of the last two millennia B.C. shows manifest shamanistic influences. The portrayal of animals in detached parts, the fighting animals, the advanced degree of abstraction in the later Sarmatian style and in the Ordos bronzes are unequivocally shamanistic. In the older rupestrian art it is above all the world-wide X-ray style that can be traced back to shamanism. The central Asian animal style affected the art of ancient China, especially that of the late Chou period, and from there extended its influence as far as Indonesia.

Shamanism's tendency to depict 'spiritual beings' led to a spiritualization, that is to say to abstraction, in art; early processes of abstraction, say in the central Asian animal style, in Tibetan art, and in rock-painting generally, must likewise be attributed to shamanism.

The Eskimo shaman Igjugarjuk to the Danish explorer Rasmussen:

'ALL TRUE WISDOM IS ONLY FOUND FAR FROM MEN, OUT IN THE GREAT SOLITUDE, AND IT CAN BE ACQUIRED ONLY THROUGH SUFFERING. PRIVATIONS AND SUFFER- INGS ARE THE ONLY THINGS THAT CAN OPEN A MAN'S MIND TO THAT WHICH IS HIDDEN FROM OTHERS.'

NOTES

INTRODUCTION

[1] Rasmussen, K., *Thulefahrt.*
[2] Knoll-Greiling, U., *Beitrag zur Psychologie.*
[3] Petri, H., *Der Australische Medizinmann.*
[4] After Knoll-Greiling, U., *Beitrag zur Psychologie.*

THE DEVELOPMENT OF THE SHAMAN

[5] Anisimov, A. F., *Predstavlenija evenkov o sinkenach i problema proischozdenija pervobitnoj religii.*
[6] Rasmussen, K., *Thulefahrt.*
[7] Rasmussen, K., *Thulefahrt,* pp. 144–5.
[8] Rasmussen, K., *Thulefahrt,* pp. 246–7.
[9] Rasmussen, K., *Thulefahrt,* p. 235.
[10] Rasmussen, K., *Thulefahrt,* pp. 237–41.
[11] Rasmussen, K., *Thulefahrt,* pp. 241–3.
[12] Schirokogorow, S. M., *Versuch einer Erforschung der Grundlagen des Schamanismus bei den Tungusen,* p. 79.
[13] Park, W. Z., *Shamanism in Western North America,* p. 25.
[14] Czaplicka, M. A., *Aboriginal Siberia,* p. 172.
[15] Mikhailovskii, V. M., *Shamanism in Siberia and European Russia.*
[16] Schirokogorow, S. M., *Versuch einer Erforschung der Grundlagen des Schamanismus bei den Tungusen,* p. 80.
[17] Radloff, W., *Aus Sibirien.*
[18] Radloff, W., *Aus Sibirien.*
[19] Schirokogorow, S. M., *Versuch einer Erforschung der Grundlagen des Schamanismus bei den Tungusen,* p. 79.
[20] Czaplicka, M. A., *Aboriginal Siberia,* p. 317.
[21] Schirokogorow, S. M., *Versuch einer Erforschung der Grundlagen des Schamanismus bei den Tungusen,* p. 76.
[22] Gmelin, F. G., *Reise durch Sibirien von dem Jahr 1733–1743.*
[23] Czaplicka, M. A., *Aboriginal Siberia,* p. 315.
[24] Prikonsky, V. L., *Das Schamanentum der Jakuten,* p. 168.
[25] Czaplicka, M. A., *Aboriginal Siberia,* pp. 314–20.
[26] Gusinde, M., *Die Feuerland-Indianer,* p. 1396.
[27] Put together after Knoll-Greiling, U., *Beitrag zur Psychologie.*
[28] Mikhailovskii, V. M., *Shamanism in Siberia and European Russia,* p. 87.
[29] Rasmussen, K., *Thulefahrt,* p. 235.
[30] Sternberg, L., *Divine Election in Primitive Religion,* p. 477.
[31] Chadwick, N. K., *Shamanism among the Tatars of Central Asia,* pp. 75–112.
[32] Russell, F., *The Pima Indians.*

33 Kroeber, A. L., *Preliminary Sketch of the Mohave Indians of California*, p. 280.
34 Park, W. Z., *Paviotso Shamanism*, p. 28.
35 Hooper, L., *The Canilla Indians*, p. 334.
36 Gusinde, M., *Die Feuerland-Indianer*, p. 1397.
37 Lowie, R. H., *The Religion of the Crow Indians*, p. 333.
38 Put together after Knoll-Greiling, U., *Beitrag zur Psychologie*.
39 Lowie, R. H., *The Religion of the Crow Indians*, p. 333.
40 Lommel, A., *Die Unambal*.

THE NATURE OF THE SHAMAN

41 Holm, H., *The Angmagsalik Eskimo*, pp. 88, 89.
42 Spier, L., *Klamath Ethnography*, p. 93.
43 Radin, P., *The Autobiography of a Winnebago Indian*, p. 19.
44 Ibid., p. 20.
45 Put together after Friedrich, A., and Buddruss, G., *Schamanengeschichten aus Sibirien*.
46 Rasmussen, K., *Thulefahrt*, pp. 240-1.
47 Waley, A., *The Nine Songs*, pp. 13, 14.
48 Put together after Friedrich, A., and Buddruss, G., *Schamanengeschichten aus Sibirien*.
49 Radloff, W., *Aus Sibirien*, p. 52.
50 Mikhailovskii, V. M., *Shamanism in Siberia and European Russia*, pp. 95, 126.
51 Jochelson, W., *Religion and Myths of the Koryaks*, p. 49.
52 Czaplicka, M. A., *Aboriginal Siberia*, p. 235.
53 Jochelson, W., *Religion and Myths of the Koryaks*, p. 51.
54 Schirokogorow, S. M., *Versuch einer Erforschung der Grundlagen des Schamanismus bei den Tungusen*, p. 74.
55 Put together after Knoll-Greiling, U., *Beitrag zur Psychologie*.

THE FUNCTION OF THE SHAMAN

56 Friedrich, A., and Buddruss, G., *Schamanengeschichten aus Sibirien*, p. 201.
57 After Lommel, A., *Die Unambal*.
58 Rasmussen, K., *Grönlandsagen*, p. 46.
59 Rasmussen, K., *Thulefahrt*, pp. 70-73.
60 After Lommel, A., *Die Unambal*.
61 Rasmussen, K., *Thulefahrt*, p. 440.
62 Rasmussen, K., *Thulefahrt*, p. 148.
63 Rasmussen, K., *Grönlandsagen*, pp. 22-27.
64 Haeberlein, H., *SbEtBtàq, A Shamanistic Performance of the Coast Salish*, 249 ff.
65 Friedrich, A., and Buddruss, G., *Schamanengeschichten aus Sibirien*.
66 Czaplicka, M. A., *Aboriginal Siberia*, p. 241.
67 After Lommel, A., *Die Unambal*.
68 After Lommel, A., *Die Unambal*.
69 After Lommel, A., *Die Unambal*.

ART AND SHAMANISM

70 Nioradze, G., *Der Schamanismus bei den sibirischen Völkern*, p. 74.
71 Nioradze, G., *Der Schamanismus bei den sibirischen Völkern*, p. 76.
72 Mikhailovskii, V. M., *Shamanism in Siberia and European Russia*, p. 84.
73 Mikhailovskii, V. M., *Shamanism in Siberia and European Russia*, p. 84.
74 Mikhailovskii, V. M., *Shamanism in Siberia and European Russia*, p. 82.
75 Nioradze, G., *Der Schamanismus bei den sibirischen Völkern*, p. 59.
76 Holmberg, U., *Siberian Mythology*.
77 Harva, U., *Die religiösen Vorstellungen der altaischen Völker*, pp. 510 ff., 525-6.
78 Schirokogorow, S. M., *Versuch einer Erforschung der Grundlagen des Schamanismus bei den Tungusen*.
79 Potapov, L. P., *Die Schamanentrommel bei den altaischen Völkerschaften*.

80 Nioradze, G., *Der Schamanismus bei den sibirischen Völkern*, p. 77.

81 Mikhailovskii, V. M., *Shamanism in Siberia and European Russia*, p. 84.

82 Nioradze, G., *Der Schamanismus bei den sibirischen Völkern*, p. 77.

83 Mikhailovskii, V. M., *Shamanism in Siberia and European Russia*, p. 81.

84 Radloff, W., *Aus Sibirien*, p. 55.

85 Put together after Knoll-Greiling, U., *Beitrag zur Psychologie*.

86 Worms, E., *Die Goranara-Feier im Australischen Kimberley*.

87 Holmberg, U., *Siberian Mythology*, p. 514.

88 Nioradze, G., *Der Schamanismus bei den sibirischen Völkern*, p. 66.

89 Nioradze, G., *Der Schamanismus bei den sibirischen Völkern*, p. 61.

90 Radloff, W., *Aus Sibirien*, p. 17.

91 Friedrich, A., and Buddruss, G., *Schamanengeschichten aus Sibirien*.

92 Schirokogorow, S. M., *Versuch einer Erforschung der Grundlagen des Schamanismus bei den Tungusen*, p. 68.

93 Nioradze, G., *Der Schamanismus bei den sibirischen Völkern*, p. 7.

94 Czaplicka, M. A., *Aboriginal Siberia*, p. 212.

95 Nioradze, G., *Der Schamanismus bei den sibirischen Völkern*, p. 66.

96 Czaplicka, M. A., *Aboriginal Siberia*, p. 213.

97 Nioradze, G., *Der Schamanismus bei den sibirischen Völkern*, p. 66.

98 Czaplicka, M. A., *Aboriginal Siberia*, p. 217.

99 Mikhailovskii, V. M., *Shamanism in Siberia and European Russia*, p. 83.

100 Put together after Knoll-Greiling, U. *Beitrag zur Psychologie*.

101 After Friedrich, A., *Knochen und Skelett*, pp. 212–13.

102 After Manker, *Die lappische Zaubertrommel*.

103 Friedrich, A., and Buddruss, G., *Schamanengeschichten aus Sibirien*.

104 Wilbert, J., *Dijubos de indios venezolanos*.

105 Lommel, A., *Die Unambal*.

LIST OF ILLUSTRATIONS

THE DRAWINGS

Page 8. Shaman beating a drum. Modern Eskimo drawing. From Miguel Covarrubias: *The Eagle, the Jaguar and the Serpent*, New York, 1954, p. 155.

Page 9. A spirit drawn by an Eskimo artist. From Rasmussen: *Thulefahrt*, Frankfurt, 1926, p. 242.

Page 11. The melancholy helping spirit Isitoq or Giant-Eye. Soon after Arnaqaoq had lost his parents this sorrowful spirit came to him and said: 'You need have no fear of me; I too struggle with sad thoughts, therefore I will follow you and be your helping spirit.' He has thick, coarse hair that stands straight up; each eye is divided into two compartments and the large mouth is vertical, with a long tooth at the top and two shorter ones at the side. His speciality is to find people who have broken the taboo. Drawing by Arnaqaoq, from Rasmussen: *Thulefahrt*, p. 247.

Page 13. Self-portrait of the shaman Arnaqaoq. From Rasmussen: *Thulefahrt*, p. 235.

Page 16. Rock-engraving from North Africa, Fezzan, Libya. From Leo Frobenius: *Ekade Ektab: Die Felsbilder Fezzans*, Leipzig, 1937, Pl. XXXIII. An ostrich hunter. What is depicted is probably not a hunting implement but hunting magic.

Page 25. Rock-engraving from North Africa, Libya. From Leo Frobenius: *Ekade Ektab: Die Felsbilder Fezzans*, Pl. IV. Representation of the ancient buffalo, *Bubalus antiquus*.

Page 26 above. Shamans in bison masks with reindeer; right, mixed creature, bison with the feet of a man, perhaps also a portrayal of a masked shaman. Trois Frères Cave, southern France. From Paola Graziosi: *Die Kunst der Altsteinzeit*, Florence, 1956, p. 276 c and d.

Page 26 below. Ostrich in a magic circle. Rock-engraving from North Africa, Libya. From Leo Frobenius: *Ekade Ektab: Die Felsbilder Fezzans*, Pl. XXXIV.

Page 27. God of the ocean, Anky-Kele, drawing from the Chukchee. From Sierksma: *Götter, Götzen and Dämonen*, Amsterdam, 1959, pp. 141-2. This drawing, made by a member of the Chukchee-Onno tribe, shows the spirit or god of the ocean surrounded by seals and whales, while a shaman approaches him, apparently to mollify the god's anger. It is a general belief among the Eskimos and the tribes of Siberia that in a state of trance the shaman leaves his body and climbs up or down to speak to the deity. Another element common to the beliefs of these peoples is the idea of a deity—sometimes a god, sometimes a goddess—who lives in the depths of the ocean, who can call forth an abundance of the animals hunted for food, and hence has power over the life and death of men. This belief is echoed in the two names by which the central Eskimos designate their Great Goddess of the ocean: the Majestic Woman and the Food Bowl. In reality these deities are the Lords or Mistresses of the Animals.

Page 28. Helping spirits which accompany the shaman on his journey into the Land of the Dead, Goldi, Siberia. From Uno Harva: *Die religiösen Vorstellungen der altaischen Völker*, Helsinki, 1938, p. 339.

Page 29. Ruler of the Whales, painted pendant from the Alaska Eskimos. From F. Sierksma: *Götter, Götzen and Dämonen*, ch. 18, p. 147. Since the portrayals of the Lord of the Animals so consistently resemble one another, there can be scarcely any doubt that the figure on the wooden pendant shown here may be regarded as a portrait of the Ruler of the Whales. The deity stands out from the rest of the drawing because it is the only figure painted in red. It is very probable that the pendant was worn during shamanistic dances held to guarantee the fertility of the animals to be hunted or to increase their numbers by supernatural intervention. Both ideas occur among hunting peoples all over the world.

It is interesting to observe that cultural influences have spread across vast distances to Siberia and Alaska.

Page 30 above. Rock-engraving from North Africa. so-called *en-face* lion. This representation was of great importance for the hunting magic of the early hunters in North Africa. From Leo Frobenius: *Hadschra Maktuba*, Pl. 46, Haju Plateau, Algeria.

Page 30 below. Rock-engraving at Tiout, North Africa. From Leo Frobenius: *Hadschra Maktuba*, Algeria. Magical scene. Perhaps a Mistress of the Animals or hunting goddess who helps hunters.

Page 31. Spirit drawn by an Eskimo artist. From Rasmussen: *Thulefahrt*, p. 251. The spirit Nujaliaq, the Hair Woman. Nose at the side of the head, thick rolls of flesh round the neck, only one arm, long, tousled hair sticking out in all directions, no body, only buttocks. The face is snow-white when it is not covered by a black leather. She carries a sealskin strap with which she catches reindeer. Speciality: she creates land animals. Drawing by Arnaqaoq.

Page 32. Spirit drawn by an Eskimo artist. From Rasmussen: *Thulefahrt*, p. 239. The sorceress Manilaq (Cake-Ice). The draughtsman met her in the summer while roaming in the mountains. She looked so terrifying that he fell down and lost consciousness and only recovered when the dog licked his navel (see top right). She became his helping spirit. Speciality: obtains animals from the Mother of the Sea Creatures. Drawing by Arnaqaoq.

Page 33. Drawing of a shaman's tent from the Evenk (Tungus). From A. F. Anisimov: *Sbornik museja antropologii i etnografii*, Vol. XII, 1949, p. 160. 'Predstavleniya evenko i problema proishoshdeniya perwobitnoy religiyi.'

Page 36. Spirit drawn by an Eskimo artist. From Rasmussen: *Thulefahrt*, p. 249. Igtuk or the Thunderer. When thunder rumbles in the mountains he is the cause of the noise. No one knows where he lives. He is made differently from all other living beings. His legs and arms are attached to the back of his body, his huge eyes are set close by his arms, while his nose has crept into his mouth. He has a bunch of thick hair on his chin and below it lie his ears. His mouth opens up into a dark gullet and when his jaws move thunder booms from inland. Drawing by Arnaqaoq.

Page 50. Drawing of a bear spirit from the Goldi, Siberia. From Uno Harva: *Die religiösen Vorstellungen der altaischen Völker*, Helsinki, 1938, III, 51.

Page 57. A shaman's skeleton from a shaman's drum, Siberia. From *Istorico Ethnographcheski Atlas Sibiri*, Moscow, 1961, p. 454, Pl. 4, Fig. 26.

Page 58. Eskimo drawing of a spirit. From Rasmussen: *Thulefahrt*, p. 245. Kigutiliq or the Spirit with the Gigantic Teeth. One day, when the artist was hunting seals, this monster rose up out of a hole cut in the ice. It was as large as a bear, but had long legs with big knots in the joints, two tails, a large ear that seemed merely to be resting in a skin-fold and teeth as huge as walrus's tusks. It gave a mighty roar and he was so frightened that he fled home without having taken the monster as a helping spirit. Drawing by Arnaqaoq.

Page 60. Drawing of a shaman with rays coming out of his head. From *Istorico Ethnographicheski Atlas Sibiri*, Moscow, 1961, p. 455, Pl. 1, Fig. 6.

Page 69. Stick with handle in the shape of a horse's head, a primitive stringed instrument used by the shaman on his journey to the other world. Buryat, Siberia. From Uno Harva: *Die religiösen Vorstellungen der altaischen Völker*, Helsinki, 1938, p. 490.

Page 70. Engraved bone from southern France, Magdalenian. From Paolo Graziosi: *Die Kunst der Altsteinzeit*, Florence, 1956, Pl. 87 d. Men in two rows; head, spine, and front legs of a bison. Probably depicts a rite for bringing a dead animal back to life.

Page 77. The Mother of the Sea Creatures, Eskimo drawing. From Rasmussen: *Thulefahrt*, p. 253. The encircled figure represents the Mother of the Sea Creatures, who sits at the bottom of the sea brooding over the destiny of men. The other drawing depicts Putuleq, the Spirit with the Many Holes. The latter shot up out of the depths of the lake while the artist was fishing for salmon. He wanted to serve a man and become his helping sprite. Speciality: helping at births. The many holes encourage the child, which comes more easily out of the mother's belly when it sees them. Drawing by Arnaqaoq.

Page 83. Eskimo drawing of spirits. From Rasmussen: *Thulefahrt*, p. 237. Two restless souls. The big one is called Nalaqnaq, the Listener; large mouth, two teeth, tongue dangling out of the mouth, shapeless hands with six fingers; moves at a run. The other is called Punqoq, Long Ear; has two mouths, three legs. One night the artist was sleeping in the shelter of a stone, when these two evil spirits fell upon him and would have devoured him if the dogs had not kept them off. Drawing by Arnaqaoq.

Page 97. Drawing of a shaman's ascent to heaven, Altai region. From Uno Harva: *Die religiösen Vorstellungen der altaischen Völker*, p. 557, Fig. 105. The thin line represents the Path of Ulgen, or the shaman's journey with his offering to the supreme god. The line leads from the tent of the presenter of the offering, where a fire is burning. Beside the path we meet first a sacrificial horse attached to a post and near it drinking-vessels: the first is intended for Bogdygan, the second for Kökysh, and the third for Ulgen. There follows a leaning stake on which the skin of the sacrificial animal is hanging. The true ascent to heaven begins beside the birch tree which, to judge by the drawing, grows inside the tent and in which the nine steps (*tapty*) have been cut. Above the birch lies Bogdygan's dwelling, in front of which we see another mythical being, Bobyrgan. Then we see nine 'swaying' places, indicated by small transverse lines. After crossing these the shaman meets Kökysh 'standing on the path to Ulgen'. Still farther on are three areas, indicated by circles, of which the first is watery and blue and the second covered in white sand; the third is so high up that even the clouds do not reach it. In the uppermost zone lives the supreme god himself, White Ulgen, surrounded by rays of light. Beside him is his 'messenger'. Of the figures which the shaman meets on his ascent to heaven, the most important are naturally those to whom the drink-offering vessels are dedicated.

Page 106. Mistress of the Animals, painting on a Greek amphora, Boeotia, seventh century B.C.

Page 107. Dancers disguised as chamois from Teyat, Dordogne, Magdalenian. From P. Graziosi: *Die Kunst der Altsteinzeit*, Florence, 1956, pp. 87 f.

Page 108. Painting of a masked, dancing shaman, Trois Frères Cave, southern France, Magdalenian. From Graziosi: *Die Kunst der Altsteinzeit*, Florence, 1956, p. 275.

Page 109 above. Drawing of a reindeer in the X-ray style from a Lapp drum. The internal organs—heart, lungs, air passage—are reduced to a thin line, the so-called 'lifeline'. From Manker: *Die lappische Zaubertrommel*, II, Uppsala, 1950, Pl. 53:9, p. 28.

Page 109 below. Head-dress of a Karagass shamaness. From Diószegi: *Glaubenswelt und Folklore der sibirischen Völker*, Budapest, 1963, Pl. 50, p. 321.

Page 110. Drawing of a spirit from northwestern Australia, Yaoro. From E. Worms: *Anali Lateranensi*, 1942, Pl. 8, p. 231.

Page 111. Shaman's coat from the Karagass. From Diószegi: *Glaubenswelt und Folklore der sibirischen Völker*, Budapest, 1963, Pl. 52, p. 323.

Page 125. Shaman's coat from the Karagass. From Diószegi: *Glaubenswelt und Folklore der sibirischen Völker*, Budapest, 1963, Pl. 51, p. 322.

Page 126. Magic rite. Shaman with drum and wolf's mask in front of a reindeer. Rock-engraving from Bessov-Noss, Lake Onega, Russia. From Bandi-Maringer: *Kunst der Eiszeit*, Basle, 1952, Pl. 198, p. 150.

Page 127. Rock-engraving. Animal in X-ray style with 'lifeline', from Evenhus, Norway. From Bandi-Maringer: *Kunst der Eiszeit*, Basle, 1952, Pl. 198, p. 150.

Page 129. Shamans fighting. Rock-painting at Lascaux, Palaeolithic. From P. Graziosi: *Die Kunst der Altsteinzeit*, Florence, 1956, p. 277.

Page 130. Rock-engraving. Reindeer, some in X-ray style, fish, sledges or boats, and symbols. Sweden, Nämforsen, Frobenius Institute, Frankfurt/M. Various epochs of the Nordic Bronze Age. An earlier phase of rock-pictures is covered by a later phase. The reindeer in X-ray style belong to the older layer.

Page 131. Rock-engraving. Cervid with internal drawing, eastern Siberia, Amur-Ussuri region.

Page 132 above. Rock-picture. Reindeer in X-ray style with meander-shaped signs. Norway, Romsdal. From Bandi-Maringer: *Kunst der Eiszeit*, Basle, 1952, Pl. 202, p. 153.

Page 132 below. Animal with 'lifeline', X-ray style. Pottery decoration of the Pueblo Indians. From F. H. Douglas and R. d'Harnoncourt: *Indian Art of the United States*, New York, 1941, p. 107.

Page 133 above. Modern Eskimo drawing. Seal in X-ray style and two-headed snake. From Miguel Covarrubias: *The Eagle, the Jaguar and the Serpent*, New York, 1954, p. 115.

Page 133 below. Kangaroo in X-ray style. Bark-drawing from Goulbourne Island, northern Australia. National Museum, Victoria.

Page 135 above. Ivory carving. Schematized female figure, Mezin, Ukraine. From Bandi-Maringer: *Kunst der Eiszeit*, Pl. 24, p. 33.

Page 135 below. Decorated sacrificial platform. Drawing on a Lapp drum. From E. Manker: *Die lappische Zaubertrommel*, Vol. II, p. 121, 4:45.

Page 136 above. Schematic representation of human ribs on an Australian wooden ritual implement.

Page 136 tentre. Decorated sacrificial platform. Drawing on a Lapp drum. From E. Manker: *Die lappische Zaubertrommel*, Vol. II, p. 121, 2:36.

Page 136 below. Human figure showing ribs, bark-engraving, Chatham Island. From C. Jeffesron: *Dendroglyphs of the Chatham Islands*, Wellington, 1956, Fig. 119.

Page 137 above. Human figure showing ribs, tattoo pattern, Marquesas. From K. v. d. Steinen: *Die Marquesaner und ihre Kunst*, Berlin, 1925, Vol. I, Fig. 121.

Page 137 centre. Human figure showing ribs, pottery decoration, China, Yang-shao (2200-1700 B.C.). From J. G. Anderson: *Researches in the Prehistory of the Chinese*, BMFEA No. 15, Stockholm, 1943, T. 182, 1.

Page 137 below. Schematic representation of a so-called thread cross from Australia.

LIST OF PLATES

1. Clay sculpture from the Magdalenian period. Le Tuc d'Audoubert, Ariège. An example of the art of the early hunters. Manifestly created as a representation of fertility, such as were produced in ever-new variations at the same period and later, almost down to our own day, in connexion with hunting magic.

2. Bark-painting from Australia from the year 1884. Representation of a 'Mistress of the Animals'. The picture comes from Field Island in northern Australia and is preserved in the South Australian Museum, Adelaide. Measurements: 117 × 38 cm. A female figure surrounded by animals is depicted in a largely geometricized style. We can see on the right a mammal, on the left a water-bird and a fish. An important fact about the picture is that the fish shows clear signs of the X-ray style. The bird and the mammal display the progressive geometricization of the X-ray style in northwestern Australia.

3. The shaman Tulayev, Karagass, Siberia. The shaman's coat and drum are in the possession of the Staatliches Museum für Völkerkunde, Munich (Mus. No. 27-48-1 a and e). The coat was acquired by Professor Petri in Irkutsk in 1927.

Professor Petri describes the Swan Costume of the Karagass as follows:

(1) Cap, consisting of green cloth with turn-up, a wolf's muzzle is depicted on the front. Above this the moon, at the sides stars. All these appliqué designs are in the white throat-hairs of the reindeer—the sacred material of which all ritual embroideries are made. Stars are also portrayed on the horns of the turn-up; the tassels are of eagle-owl's feathers, the feathers of a bird known as *kedrovka* and squirrels' tails—these are the shaman's helping animals. The lower edge is of sable fur, replaced at the back by sheepskin (this is an innova-tion, because they have to buy sheepskin from the Buryat). The long ribbon at the back of the cap also bears star designs. It represents the shaman's spine; the stars are a symbol for heaven. The white shaman Tulayev is under the protection of heavenly spirits and bears their symbols.

(2) The drum consists of a wooden frame covered with deerskin (*Cervus canadensis*). Between skin and frame there are rattles (resonators). Karagass drums do not have drawings on them. The handle of the drum is attached in the direction of its greatest diameter; there are no drawings here either. From the handle four transverse pieces of wood run to the frame. In the upper part the frame carries two metal arcs (called *kulak* ears) to which iron rattles are attached. With the aid of these 'ears' the shaman hears the voices of the spirits. The ribbons attached to them are gifts from those who believe in the shaman's guardian spirits. When a karagass invites a shaman he must first hang one of these ribbons (called *dzalama*) on his drum. The long strings are also *dzalama*, but the shaman himself has put them on his drum in honour of his guardian spirit.

(3) The drumstick is a piece of reindeer horn (*Ragnifer tarandus*) and is covered with skin from the same animal's foot. The drumstick is also the knout with which the shaman drives the animal on which he rides (i.e. the shaman's soul rides on the soul of the animal whose skin is stretched on the drum). So that the drum-stick cannot fall to the ground during the ceremony it is tied to a loop.

(4) The coat is made from the skin of a fully grown reindeer (*Ragnifer tarandus*); only the chest is made from the skin of a three- or four-months-old reindeer calf. In the front are strips of blue Chinese fabric. The vertical strip is the breastbone, those on either side are the ribs, the strings are the nipples. The cross on the chest, the shaman explained to me, merely means that he, too—like a Christian priest—is a servant of religion and as such can also wear a cross.

The vertical embroidery on the back represents the spine. The ribs go out from it. The arm bones are like-wise embroidered on the sleeves. When the shaman puts on this costume he becomes a creature with an unusual skeleton: the hostile spirits cannot do anything to his bones. On his shoulders are two bunches of eagle-owl's feathers: these are the shaman's wings. He can fly with them when the course of the ritual demands it. Between his shoulder-blades hangs a metal hoop with rattles. When the shaman notices the approach of evil spirits he shakes himself, so that the rattles make a noise. Then the spirits are frightened by the noise of iron and flee. The many thick strings are snakes. They are relations of the *jutba*, the monstrous snake that guards the entrance to the underworld, where Erlyn-Khan (Erlik), the terrible devouring god, lives. With the aid of his snakes the shaman is able to force his way into Erlik's dwelling. The other appendages on the back are two leather caps, caps of invisibility; with their help the shaman can escape the evil spirits which pursue him. All the other appendages—ribbons, strings, etc—represent *dzalama* dedicated to the shaman's various guardian spirits. Every shaman makes his costume according to the instructions of the spirits which appear to him in a dream and tell him how to make it. Moreover, he is also helped by the old men who remember what kind of costume the shaman's father or grandfather had, assuming that the latter were shamans.

(5) Boots of reindeer leather; the embroidery on them represents the leg and toe bones.

Professor Petri was in Irkutsk in 1927. The shaman's costume was sent by Petri from Irkutsk to the German Consulate at Novosibirsk. The Consulate then sent it on via Moscow to Berlin.

4. The Eskimo shaman Najagneq from the island of Nunivak. The photograph was taken in 1924 during the fifth Danish expedition to Thule under the leadership of Knut Rasmussen. It was the shaman Najagneq who gave the definition of a shaman on page 1.

5. Doll from northwest America. Wood with movable limbs. The doll represents a spirit of the dead. Such dolls were used by the shamans during the performance of secret myths. Royal Ontario Museum, Canada. Cat. Seattle World's Fair 1962, *Northwest Coast Indian Art*, No. 156.

6, 7. Figure of a bear with small human figure. In this way the relationship of a man or a shaman to his guardian spirit was portrayed. Northwest America. Kwakiutl tribe. Collected between 1895 and 1901. Private collection. Cat. Seattle World's Fair 1962, *Northwest Coast Indian Art*, No. 125.

8. Small wooden figure of a singing shaman. Since parts of the skeleton are visible, we may assume that the shaman is portrayed as a dead man in the next world or during the initiation ceremony, the process of 'being cut up'. Princeton University Museum of Geology and Palaeontology. Cat. Seattle World's Fair 1962, *Northwest Coast Indian Art*, No. 4.

9. Thirteenth-century Chinese picture, *Ascent to Heaven*, painted by Yen Hui in light colours on silk. Preserved in the Chion-yi Monastery, Kyoto, Japan. The picture shows the Taoist saint Li (Li-t'ieh-kuai). The holy Li was able to ride through the air and up to heaven when he wished to converse with Master Laotse. On one occasion he was unable to find his body on his return to earth and slipped into the body of a beggar who had just died, and thereafter wandered about the country with the latter's crutches, every now and then—as in this picture—sending his figure to heaven. In this picture the ancient shamanistic idea of the 'journey to heaven and the other world' is still depicted in the thirteenth century A.D. Illustration from *du-atlantis*, August 1964, Werner Speiser: *Beispiele Altchinesischer Malerei*.

10. Two wildly dancing shamans. The pictures in a fifteenth-century Turkish manuscript take us straight into the unadulterated spiritual atmosphere of shamanism. We see spirits and dancing shamans. (See Plates 10, 11, 12, 13, and 15.)

The manuscript (Fatih Album) from which the pictures are taken was drawn by Ustat Memhed Siyah Kalem, known as the Black Feather. There are virtually no forerunners for the style of this artist within Islamic art. He manifestly drew his inspiration from the Chinese Yüan period (1280–1368) or the early Ming period (1368–1664). The pictures are preserved in the Topkapi Museum, Istanbul.

11. Cowering demon (detail).

12. Spirits who have torn to pieces the body of a horse and are fighting over their prey.

13. Two demons fighting.

14. Wooden doll forming part of a shaman's equipment. Alaska, before 1890. Museum of the American Indian, Heye Foundation, New York. From Dockstader: *Kunst in America*, I, Stuttgart, Belser Verlag.

15. A shaman dancing with spirits.

16. Small wooden figure of a dead shaman in the process of travelling to the 'next world' in a trance. North-west America, Haida tribe. Princeton University of Geology and Palaeontology. Cat. Seattle World's Fair 1962, *Northwest Coast Indian Art*, No. 6.

17. Shaman's coat from the Tungus, from the Göttingen University Collection (Museum für Völker-kunde, Göttingen). The coat dates from the second half of the eighteenth century. Belonging to the coat are a

copper mask, a Chinese metal mirror and several small copper masks, as well as iron figurines of animals and men, small dolls and the like. All these objects symbolize the shaman's helping spirits.

18. Rear view of the Tungus shaman's coat. The various appendages may be clearly seen.

19. Iron doll and rudimentary mask from the Tungus shaman's coat of Pl. 17. In this costume a great deal of copper is used in the masks. This is not usual; in Siberia the appendages and masks attached to shamans' coats are mostly of iron, as the small doll shows.

20. Detail of the shaman's coat of Pl. 17. The three metal figures represent helping gods.

21. Two masks from the Tungus shaman's coat of Pl. 17. Likewise representations of helping gods.

22. Painted Canadian Indian shaman's rattle. Staatl. Museum für Völkerkunde, Munich, Mus. No. 26–3–34. Besides a number of uninterpretable geometrical signs, the rattle is decorated with two eagles. In North America, among the Indians and the Eskimos, the eagle plays an important role, as the bird which brought men the mysteries, magic, and feasts.

23. Shaman's mask of wood. It represents Walaunuk, the spirit of rising bubbles. Kuskokwim River, Alaska, before 1900. (Ref. see Pl. 14.)

24. Painted shaman's drum. Staatl. Museum für Völkerkunde, Munich, no number. Probably North American origin. The painting on the drum is geometrical. It is divided into fields, in each field a kind of sun. Comparisons with Siberian drums might lead us to interpret diagonal strokes at the four ends of the cross as an abstract face.

25. Shaman's mask. Spirit of the seal. Kuskokwim River, Alaska, before 1900. (Ref. see Pl. 14.)

26. Shaman's mask, representing a 'cold-weather spirit'. The masks were ritually burned at the beginning of spring. Kuskokwim River, Alaska, before 1900. (Ref. see Pl. 14.)

27. Two metal masks and fabric dolls from a Tungus shaman's coat (Pl. 17). Masks and dolls represent helping spirits.

28. Painted mask from the Eskimos of southwest Alaska. The mask represents a spirit, perhaps a helping spirit, as it appears to the shaman in a trance. The mask is typical of Eskimo art arising from visions. Museum of Anthropology, University of California, Berkeley.

29. Shaman's mask, representing the spirit of the octopus. Northwest America, Kwakiutl region, before 1900. (Ref. see Pl. 14.)

30. Hinged shaman's mask. These masks could be opened during the ceremony. Under the first, outer face there appeared a second. This symbolized the dual nature of a spirit. British Columbia, between 1830 and 1875. (Ref. see Pl. 14.)

31. Small mask of wood, representing a helping spirit. Alaska, before 1890. (Ref. see Pl. 14.)

32. Small mask of walrus ivory, representing a helping spirit. Alaska, before 1875. (Ref. see Pl. 14.)

33. Shaman's mask. Fabulous animal holding a seal in its jaws, representing a helping spirit. Alaska, before 1900. (Ref. see Pl. 14.)

34. Handle of a shaman's drum of walrus ivory. Alaska, before 1900. (Ref. see Pl. 14.)

35. Ritual utensil of a shaman. In a boat in the shape of a sea serpent seven helping spirits, depicted as crouching ancestor figures, are coming to the aid of the shaman. Northwest America, Tlingit, before 1875. (Ref. see Pl. 14.)

36. A shaman's double mask. Here, too, a spirit being is portrayed in two different forms. Northwest America, before 1900. (Ref. see Pl. 14.)

37. Helping spirit in the shape of a raven's head in the interior of which human faces, further helping spirits, have been carved. Northwest America, Tlingit, before 1875. (Ref. see Pl. 14.)

38. Shaman's mask, representing the brown bear. Alaska, before 1850. (Ref. see Pl. 14.)

39. A so-called 'soul-catcher', an instrument used in shamanist rituals to bring back the souls of people seriously ill. The little work of art shows a two-headed snake, a mythical symbol known throughout the Arctic, especially in America. (Ref. see Pl. 14.)

40. Shaman's mask with tufts of human hair attached. The artistic quality of this mask is exceptional. Found on the Skeena River, British Columbia, c. 1600. (Ref. see Pl. 14.)

41. Shaman's drum from the Lapps. Staatl. Museum für Völkerkunde, Munich, Mus. No. 5783. This drum is mentioned as long ago as 1801 as being in the possession of the University of Altdorf near Nuremberg, and illustrated, by Christoph Gottlieb von Murr: *Beschreibung der vornehmsten Merkwürdigkeiten in der Reichsstadt Nürnberg, in deren Bezirke und auf der Universität Altdorf nebst einem Anhange.* Second enlarged edition. With a copperplate. Nuremberg, 1801. Ernst Manker refers to the drum at length as No. 68 in his book *Die lappische Zaubertrommel*, Vol. I, Pl. 31, p. 54, and in Vol. II, Pl. 150, p. 424. The painting on the drum is divided into three fields: upper world, underworld, and middle zone. The important thing about the drum is that at

least two of the animal figures show clear traces of the X-ray style. The meaning of the design is explained at length by Manker.

42. Shaman's mask. A whole group of helping spirits—seal, bear, walrus, stag, and reindeer—are combined in this mask. From Alaska, dates from between 1875 and 1900. (Ref. see Pl. 14.)

43. Shaman's mask. Combination of an animal, a wolf, and its victim, a man. Northwest America, Kwakiutl region, before 1900. (Ref. see Pl. 14.)

44. Shaman's mask. One half represents a seal; the other the seal's spirit, *inua*. Alaska, before 1910. (Ref. see Pl. 14.)

BIBLIOGRAPHY

Agapitow, N. N.; Changalow, M. N. 'Beiträge zur Kenntniß des Schamanismus in Sibirien. I. Das Schamanenthum unter den Burjäten des Gouvern. Irkutsk.' Spec. repr.: *Nachrichten der Ostsibirischen Abth. d. k. Russ. Georg. Ges. in Irkutsk*, Bd. XIV, 1883, s. *Globus*, Vol. 52, pp. 250-3, 268-70, 286-8, 299-301, 316-18.

Agapitoff, N. N.; Changolow, M. N. *Materials for the Study of Shamanism in Siberia.* E. S. S. L. R. 6 S. Irkutsk, 1883 (Russian), Irkutsk, 1883.

Alexander, H. B. *The Mythology of all Races*, Vol. X, North American, Boston, 1916.

Alexejenko, J. A. 'Der Bärenkult der Keten (Yenissei-Ostyakr)', *Glaubenswelt und Folklore der sibirischen Völker*, pp. 191-208, Budapest, 1963.

Andres, F. 'Die Himmelsreise der caraïbischen Medizinmänner', *Zeitschrift für Ethnologie*, Bd. 70, pp. 331-43, Berlin, 1939.

Anisimov, A. F. 'Cosmological Concepts of the Peoples of the North', *Studies in Siberian Shamanism*, pp. 157-229, Toronto, 1963.

Anisimov, A. F. 'Predstavlenija evenkov o sinkenach i problema proishoschdenija pervobitnoj religiji', *Sbornik museja antropologiji i etnografiji*, Vol. XII, p. 160, Leningrad, 1949.

Anisimov, A. F. *The Shaman's Tent of the Evenks and the Origin of the Shamanistic Rite Studies in Siberian Shamanism*, pp. 84-123, Toronto, 1963.

Anochin, A. *Die Vorstellungen von der Seele bei den teleutischen Schamanisten in Altai.* Résumé deutsch, Text Russian. Publ. Musée d'Anthrop., 8, pp. 268-9, 333, Bemerkung von Malov, Leningrad, 1929.

Anochin, A. B. 'Materialii po šamanstvu u Altaitsev, Sborn', *Museja Antrop. i Etnogr. Ross. Ak. Nauk. T.*, IV, 2, Leningrad, 1924.

Anutschin, V. J. *Skizze des Schamanismus der Jenissei Ostjaken*, Pub. Musée Anthr. et Ethnogr. Acad. Imp. Sciences Petersburg, Vol. II, No. 2, St Petersburg, 1914.

Awrorin, W. A. 'Ein nanajisches (goldisches) Märchen vom vierzigsten Bruder und seiner Frau, der Waschbärin', *Glaubenswelt und Folklore der sibirischen Völker*, pp. 405-14, Budapest, 1963.

Bálazs, J. 'Über die Ekstase des ungarischen Schamanen', *Glaubenswelt und Folklore der sibirischen Völker*, pp. 57-83, Budapest, 1963.

Barandiaran, D. de. 'Shamanismo Yekuana o Makiritare', *Antropológica*, No. 11, pp. 61-90, Caracas, 1962.

Barry, Ph. 'The Bridge of Sunbeams', *Journal of American Folklore*, Vol. 27, pp. 79-89, 1914.

Bastian, Adolf. 'Ein Besuch bei einem burjätischen Schamanen', *Geographische und ethnologische Bilder*, Jena, 1873.

Baumann, H. *Afrikanische Wild- und Busch-geister*, Festschrift für B. Ankermann, Berlin, 1939.

Baumann, H. 'Das Tier als Alter Ego in Afrika', *Paideuma*, Vol. 5, pp. 157-66, Wiesbaden, 1952.

Baumann, H. *Das doppelte Geschlecht*, Berlin, 1955.

Beal, Samuel. *The life of Hiuen Tsiang by the Shaman Hwui Li*, London, 1911.

Beasley, H. G. 'A Memorial Figure of a Haida Shaman', *Man*, Vol. 35, Art. 126, p. 113, London, 1935.

Beck, Paul Ekstase. *Beitrag zur Psychologie und Völkerkunde*, Leipzig, 1923.

Benedict, Ruth Fulton. 'The Vision in Plains Culture', *American Anthropologist*, Vol. 24, 1922.

Benedict, Ruth Fulton. *The Concept of the Guardian Spirit in North America*, American Anthropological Association—Memoir No. 29, 1923.

Bernštam, A. N. 'Nashalnye izobraženija Sajmaly Taš', *Sovetskaja Etnografija*, No. 2, pp. 50–68, 1952.

Bilz, Rudolf. *Pars pro toto*, Leipzig, 1940.

Birket-Smith, Kay. *The Eskimos*, London, 1936.

Bleichsteiner, Robert. *Die gelbe Kirche. Mysterien der buddhistischen Klöster in Indien, Tibet, Mongolei und China*, Vienna, 1937.

Boas, Franz. 'The Central Eskimos', *Ann. Rep. Bur. Ethnology*, Vol. 6, 1884–5, Washington, 1888.

Boas, Franz. *The Social Organisation and the Secret Societies of the Kwakiutl Indians*, Washington, 1897.

Boas, Franz. 'The Eskimos of Baffinland and Hudson Bay', *Amer. Mus. of Nat. Hist. Bull.*, Vol. XV, 1907.

Bober, P. P. Cernunnos. 'Origin and Transformation of a Celtic Divinity', *American Journal of Archaeology*, Vol. 55, pp. 13–51, 1951.

Bogoras, Waldemar, 'The Cukchee', Publ. of J.N.P.E., Vol. VII, Mem. of the American Museum of Natural History, Jesup North Pacific Expedition, New York, 1904–10.

Bogoras, Waldemar. 'K psichologi chamanstwan narodow sewo o wostotschnog Asii', *Ent. Obosrengo*, Moskva, 1910.

Bornemann, F. 'Zum Form- und Quantitäts-kriterium', *Anthropos*, No. 33, pp. 614–50, 1938.

Bouteiller, Marcelle. 'Don chamanistique et adaptation à la vie chez les Indiens de l'Amérique du Nord', *Journ. de la Soc. d. Americanistes*, N.S., Vol. XXXIX, pp. 1–14, Paris, 1950.

Buber, Martin. 'Ekstatische Konfessionen', *Archiv für Religionswissenschaften*, No. 19.

Bulck, P. G. van. *Beiträge zur Methodik der Völkerkunde* (Wiener Beiträge zur Kulturgeschichte und Linguistik, No. 2), Vienna, 1931.

Butt, Audrey J. 'Ritual blowing', *Man*, Vol. 56, Art. 48, pp. 49–55, Pl. D, London, 1956.

Canto, Borges do. 'A pesca na Lagoa Panguila e defumaçaõ do peixe', *Estudos Etnográfikos*, I, S.

Casanowicz, I. M. 'Shamanism of the Natives of Siberia', *Ann. Rep. Board of Regents 1924*, pp. 415–34, Washington, 1924.

Chadwick, Nora K. 'Shamanism among the Tatars of Central Asia', *Journal of the Royal Anthropological Institute of Great Britain and Ireland*, Vol. LXVI, pp. 75–112, London, 1936.

Chamberlain, A. F. 'Rootenay "Medicine Man"', *Journal of American Folk-Lore*, Vol. 14, 1901.

Charles, L. H. 'Drama in Shaman Exorcism', *Journal of American Folk-Lore*, No. 66, pp. 95–122, 1953.

Chernetsov, V. N. 'Concepts of the Soul among the Ob Ugrians', *Studies in Siberian Shamanism*, pp. 3–45, Toronto, 1963.

Clark, J. G. D. *Excavation at Star Carr, An Early Mesolithic Site at Seamer near Scarborough, Yorkshire*, Cambridge, U.P., 1954.

Clements, Forest E. *Primitive Concepts of Disence*, Univ. of California, Publ. in Amer. Arch. and Ethnology, Vol. 32, 1932.

Closs, A. 'Historische Ethnologie und Germanistik', *Anthropos*, No. 51, pp. 833–91, Fribourg, 1956.

Coe, Michael D. 'Shamanism in the Bunun tribe, Central Formosa', *Ethos*, Vol. 20, No. 4, pp. 181–98, Stockholm, 1955.

Czaplicka, Marie Antoinette. *Aboriginal Siberia*, Oxford, 1914.

Deroy, L. 'La sandale ailée et l'origine Hittite du dieu Hermès', *Athenaeum*, N. S., Vol. 30, pp. 59–84, 1952.

Diószegi, V. 'A viaskodó táltosbika és a sámán állatalakú életlelke', *Ethnographie*, Vol. 63, pp. 308–57, 1952.

Diószegi, V. 'K voprosu o bor'be šamanov v obraze žívotnych', *Acta Orientalia Hungarica*, Vol. 2, pp. 303–16, 1953.

Diószegi, V. 'Golovnyj ubor nanajskich (goldskich) šamanov', *Néprajzi Értesíte*, Vol. 37, pp. 81–103, 1955.

Diószegi, V. 'Die Überreste des Schamanismus in der ungarischen Volkskultur', *Acta Ethnographica*, Vol. 7, pp. 97–134, 1958.

Diószegi, V. 'Zum Problem der ethnischen Homogenität des tofischen (karagassischen) Schamanismus', *Glaubenswelt und Folklore der sibirischen Völker*, pp. 261–357, Budapest, 1963.

Diószegi, V. 'Die Drei-Stufen-Amulette der Nanajen (Golden)', *Glaubenswelt und Folklore der sibirischen Völker*, pp. 415–36, Budapest, 1963.

Diseelhoff, H. D. 'Bemerkungen zu einigen Eskimo-Masken der Sammlung Jacobsen des Berliner Museums f. Völkerkunde', *Baessler-Archiv*, 18, Berlin, 1935.

Dittrich, Edith. 'Das Motiv des Tierkampfes in der altchinesischen Kunst', *Asiatische Forschungen*, No. 13, Wiesbaden, 1963.

Dixon, Roland B. 'Some Shamans of Northern California', *Journal of American Folk-Lore*, Vol. 17, 1904.

Dixon, Roland B. 'The Northern Maidu', *Amer. Mus. of Nat. Hist. Bull.*, 17, Part 3, 1905.

Dixon, Roland B. 'The Shasta', *Amer. Mus. of Nat. Hist. Bull.*, 17, Part 5, 1907.

Dixon, Roland B. 'Some Aspects of the American Shaman', *Journal of American Folk-lore*, Vol. 21, 1908.

Dockstader, Frederick J. *Kunst in America*, I, Stuttgart, 1965.

Dorsey, George. *The Arapaho Sun Dance*, Chicago, 1903.

Dorsey, George. 'Traditions of the Skidi Pawnee', *Memoirs of American Folklore Society*, Vol. 26, 1904.

Dyrenkova, N. P. *L'obtention du don chamanique selon les idées des tribus turques* (*Polucenie samanskogo dara po vozzrenijam tureckich plemen*) *Sbornik Muzeja Antropologii i Etnografi* (*Archiv des Museum für Anthropologie und Ethnographie*), Vol. IX, Academy of Sciences of the U.S.S.R., pp. 267-91, Leningrad, 1930.

Dyrenkowa, N. P. 'Kinderschutz bei den Schoren', *Glaubenswelt und Folklore der sibirischen Völker*, pp. 257-9, Budapest, 1963.

Eder, Matthias. 'Schamanismus in Japan', *Paideuma*, Vol. VI, No. 7, pp. 367-80, Wiesbaden, 1958.

Egede, Paul. *Nachrichten aus Grönland*, Kopenhagen, 1790.

Elkin, A. P. 'Aboriginal Men of High Degree', *The John Murtagh Macrossan Memorial Lectures for 1944*, Australasian Publishing Co., Sydney, 1945.

Eliade, M. 'Einführende Betrachtungen über den Schamanismus', *Paideuma*, Vol. 5, pp. 87-97, Bamberg, 1951.

Eliade, M. 'Techniques de l'extase et langages secrets', Estratto dal II Vol. di 'Conferenze' Istituto Italiano per il Medio ed Estremo Oriente, Rome, 1953.

Eliade, M. 'Expérience sensorielle et expérience mystique chez les primitifs', Extrait des Études Carmélitaines pp. 70-99, no place, no date.

Eliade, Mircea. *Schamanismus und archaische Ekstasetechnik*, Zürich/Stuttgart, 1957.

Eliade, Mircea. 'Spiritual Thread, Sūtrātman, Catena Aurea', *Paideuma*, Vol. VII, No. 4/6, pp. 225-34, Wiesbaden, 1960.

Elwin, Verrier. *The Religion of an Indian Tribe*, London, 1955.

Emmonds, G. T. V.; Miles, G. P. L. 'Shamanistic Charms', *Ethnologia Cramorensis*, Vol. 4, pp. 31-35, 1935.

Emsheimer, E. 'Schamanentrommel und Trommelbaum', *Ethnos*, Vol. II, No. 4, pp. 166-81, Stockholm, 1945.

Emsheimer, E. 'Eine sibirische Parallele zur lappischen Zaubertrommel', *Ethnos*, Vol. 13, 1-2, pp. 17-26, Stockholm, 1948.

Erman, Georg Adolf. *Reisen um die Erde durch Nordasien 1828-30*, Berlin, 1839.

Evans, E. J. 'Mycenaean Tree and Pillar Cult and Its Mediterranean Relations', *Journal of Hellenic Studies*, Vol. 21, pp. 99-204, 1901.

Evans-Wentz, W. Y. 'Psychol. Kommenta von C. G. Jung', *Das tibetanische Totenbuch*, Leipzig, 1935.

Findeisen, Hans. 'Schamanentum im tungusischen Kinderspiel', *Zeitschrift für Ethnologie*, Vol. 78, No. 2, pp. 307-8, Braunschweig, 1953.

Findeisen, Hans. *Schamanentum*, Urban Bücher No. 28, Stuttgart, 1957.

Findeisen, Hans. 'Das Schamanentum als spiritistische Religion', *Ethnos*, Vol. 25, pp. 192-213, Stockholm, 1960.

Firth, Raymond. 'Problem and Assumption in an Anthropological Study of Religion', *Journal of the Royal Anthr. Inst.*, Vol. 89, No. 2, pp. 129-48, London, 1959.

Freeland, L. S. *Pomo Doctors and Poisoners*, Univ. of California, Publ. in American Archaeology and Ethnology, Vol. 20, 1923.

Friedrich, A. 'Die Forschung über das frühzeitliche Jägertum', *Paideuma*, Vol. 2, pp. 20-43, Leipzig, 1941.

Friedrich, A. 'Knochen und Skelett in der Vorstellungswelt Norsasiens', *Wiener Beiträge zur Kulturgeschichte und Linguistik*, Vol. 5, pp. 189-247, Vienna, 1943-4.

Friedrich, A.; Buddruss, G. *Schamanengeschichten aus Sibirien*, München-Planegg, 1955.

Frobenius, Leo. *Erlebte Erdteile*, I-VII, Frankfurt/M., 1925-9.

Frobenius, L. 'Das Archiv für Folkloristik', *Paideuma*, Vol. I, pp. 1–19, Leipzig, 1938.

Gahs, A. 'Blutige und unblutige Opfer bei den altaiischen Hirtenvölkern', *International Week for the Ethnology of Religions, Milan, 1925*, pp. 217–32, Paris, 1926.

Gáldi, L. 'Zu einigen Problemen des Versbaus in den samojedischen Schamanengesängen', *Glaubenswelt und Folklore der sibirischen Völker*, pp. 135–47, Budapest, 1963.

Gayton, A. H. *Yokuts-Mono Chiefs and Shamans*, Univ. of California, Publ. in American Archaeology and Ethnology, Vol. 24, No. 8, 1930.

Gmelin, F. G. *Reise durch Sibirien von dem Jahr 1733–1734*, Göttingen, 1751.

Goddard, Pliny Earl. *Life and Culture of the Hupa*, Univ. of California, Publ. in American Archaeology and Ethnology, Vol. 1, No. 1, 1903.

Goltz, v.d. Zauberei und Hexenkünste. 'Spiritismus und Schamanismus in China', *Mitt. Tokyo*, Vol. 6, pp. 1–36.

Graebner, F. *Die Methode der Ethnologie*, Heidelberg, 1922.

Grinnel, George Bird. 'The Great Mysteries of the Cheyenne', *American Anthropologist*, Vol. XII, 1910.

Grube, Wilhelm. 'Das Schamanentum bei den Golden', *Globus*, Vol. LXXI, pp. 89–93, Braunschweig, 1897.

Grünwedel, Albert. 'Mythologie des Buddhismus in Tibet und der Mongolei', *Führer durch die lamaistische Sammlung des Fürsten E. Uchtomskij*, Leipzig, 1900.

Gunda, B. 'Totemistische Spuren in der ungarischen táltos-Überlieferung', *Glaubenswelt und Folklore der sibirischen Völker*, pp. 45–56, Budapest, 1963.

Gurian, N. N. 'Pamjatniki epochi rannego metalla na severnom proberež'e Kolskogo poluostrova', *Materialy i Issledovanija po Archeologii SSSR*, No. 39, pp. 347–407, 1953.

Gusinde, Martin. *Die Feuerland-Indianer*, Vol. I, II, Mödling bei Wien, 1937.

Haberlandt, A. 'Der Aufbau der europäischen Volkskultur', *Die Große Völkerkunde*, Vol. I, pp. 59–72, Leipzig, 1939.

Haeberlin, Hermann. 'SbEtBtàq, A Shamanistic Performance of the Coast Salish', *American Anthropologist*, Vol. 20, 1918.

Haekel, J. 'Idolkult und Dualsystem bei den Ugriern', *Archiv für Völkerkunde*, Vol. I, pp. 95–163, Vienna, 1946.

Haekel, J. 'Die Vorstellung vom Zweiten Ich in den amerikanischen Hochkulturen', *Wiener Beiträge zur Kulturgeschichte und Linguistik*, Vol. 9, pp. 124–88, Vienna, 1952.

Hajdú, Von der. 'Klassifikation der samojedischen Schamenen', *Glaubenswelt und Folklore der sibirischen Völker*, pp. 161–90, Budapest, 1963.

Hallowell, I. 'Bear Ceremonialism in the Northern Hemisphere', *American Anthropologist*, Vol. 28.

Handbook of American Indians. Bureau of American Ethnology, Bulletin, Vol. 30, 1910.

Harper, E. B. 'Shamanism in South India', *Southwestern Journal of Anthropology*, Vol. 13, pp. 267–87.

Harrington, M. R. 'A Preliminary Sketch of Lenape Culture', *American Anthropologist*, Vol. 15, 1913.

Hartwig, Werner. 'Gedanken über ein Schamanenkostüm (nach Notizen von J. A. Jewsenin)', *Jahrb. d. Mus. f. Völkerkunde zu Leipzig*, Vol. XV, 1956, pp. 37–50, Leipzig, 1957.

Hartwig, W. 'Beschwörend dröhnt die Trommel durch die Nacht', *Mitt. aus dem Museum für Völkerkunde zu Leipzig*, No. 7, pp. 7–9, Leipzig, 1961.

Harva, U. *Die religiösen Vorstellungen der altaiischen Völker* (Folklore Fellows Comm. No. 125), Helsinki, 1938.

Hastings, James (Ed.). *Encyclopaedia of Religion and Ethics*, 13 vols., New York, 1908–21.

Hatt, G. 'Asiatic influences in American Folklore', *Det Kongelige Danske Videnskabernes Selskabs Skrifter*, Vol. 31, No. 6, Copenhagen, 1949.

Hauer, Jakob Wilhelm. *Die Religionen, ihr Werden, ihr Sinn, ihre Wahrheit*, Stuttgart, 1923.

Heissig, Walther. 'A Mongolian Source to the Lamist Suppression of Shamanism in the 17th Century', *Anthropos*, Vol. 48, pp. 1–29, 493–536, Fribourg, 1953.

H., C. 'Eine Schamanenvorstellung', *Globus*, Vol. 48, pp. 168–269, Braunschweig, 1885.

Hentze, C. 'Schamanenkronen zur Han-Zeit in Korea', *Ostasiatische Zeitschrift*, Vol. 19, 5, pp. 156–63, 1933.

Hentze, Ca. 'Eine Schamanendarstellung auf einem Han-Relief', *Asia Major*, N.F., Vol. I, pp. 74–77, Leipzig and Vienna, 1944.

Hentze, Carl. 'Eine Schamanentracht in ihrer Bedeutung für die altchinesische Kunst', *Ipek*, Vol. 20, pp. 55–61, Berlin, 1963.

Hodge, Frederic Webb (Ed.). *Handbook of American Indians, North of Mexico*. Bulletin, Vol. 30, Bureau of American Ethnology, 1907.

Hoffmann, H. *Quellen zur Geschichte der tibetanischen Bon-Religion*, Akademie der Wissenschaften und der Literatur, *Abhandlungen der Geistes- und Sozial-wissenschaftlichen Klasse, Jahrg*, 1950, No. 4, Wiesbaden, 1950.

Hoffmann, H. *Die Religionen Tibets*, München, 1956.

Hoffman, W. J. *The Midewewen or 'Grand Medicine Society'*, Bureau of American Ethnology, Annual Reports, Vol. VII, 1885–6.

Hoffman, W. J. 'Schamanentum bei den Ojibwa und Menomoni', *Globus*, Vol. 61, pp. 92–95, Braunschweig, 1892.

Holm, G. 'The Angmagsalik Eskimos', *Medd. om Grönland*, Copenhagen, 1914.

Holmberg, Uno. *Siberian Mythology*, Boston, 1927.

Holmer, N. M.; Wassén, S. H. 'Dos cantos shamanisticos de los indios Cunas', *Etnologiska Studier*, No. 127, Göteborg, 1963.

Hooke, S. H. 'Some Parallels with the Gilgamesh Story, The Siege Perilous', *Essays in Biblical Anthropology*, pp. 51–65, London, 1956.

Hooper, Lucille. *The Cannilla Indians*. Univ. of California, Publ. in American Archaeology and Ethnology, Vol. 16, No. 6, 1920.

Horneffer, August. *Symbolik der Mysterienbünde*, Munich, 1916.

Huizinga. *Homo ludens*, Amsterdam, 1939.

Hultkrantz, A. *The North American Indian Orpheus Tradition*, The Ethnographical Museum of Sweden, Monograph Series, Publication No. 2, Stockholm, 1957.

Israel, Heinz. 'Der Schamanismus bei den Völkern Sibiriens am Objekt erläutert', *Dresdener Wiss. Mus.*, pp. 152–60, Dresden, 1956.

Ivanov, S. I. *Materialy po izobrazitel' nomu iskusstvu narodov Sibiri XIX načala XX v. Trudy Instituta Etnografi*, N.A., Vol. 22, Leningrad, 1954.

Jarring, Gunnar. 'A Note on Shamanism in Eastern Turkestan', *Ethnos*, Vol. 26, pp. 1–4, Stockholm, 1961.

Jaspers, Karl. *Allgemeine Psychopathologie*. Berlin, 1913.

Jensen, Ad. E. 'Über das Töten als kulturgeschichtliche Erscheinung', *Paideuma*, Vol. 4, pp. 23–38, Bamberg, 1950.

Jettmar, K. 'Archäologische Spuren von Indogermanen in Zentralasien', *Paideuma*, Vol. 5, pp. 236–54, Bamberg, 1952.

Jettmar, Karl. *Die frühen Steppenvölker*, Baden-Baden, 1964.

Jochelson, Waldemar. *Religion and Myths of the Koryaks*, Publ. of Jesup North Pacific Expedition, Vol. VI, Memoir of the American Museum of Natural History, 10, Leiden/New York, 1905–8.

Jochelson, Waldemar. *The Yugakir*, Vol. II, Jesup North Pacific Expedition, Vol. IX.

Jung, C. G. *Psychologische Typen*, Zürich, 1921.

Jung, C. G. *Wandlungen und Symbole der Libido*, Leipzig, 1938.

Jung, C. G. *Psychologie und Religion*, Zürich, 1940.

Jung, C. G.; Kerenyi, K. *Einführung in das Wesen der Mythologie*, Leipzig, 1941.

Junod, Henry. *Life of South African Tribe*, Neuchatel, 1912.

Jussupow, G. W. 'Totemistische Relikte bei den Kasaner Tataren', *Glaubenswelt und Folklore der sibirischen Völker*, pp. 209–22, Budapest, 1963.

Kálmán, B. 'Zwei Reinigungsriten im Bärenkult der Obugrier', *Glaubenswelt und Folklore der sibirischen Völker*, pp. 93–100, Budapest, 1963.

Kelly, Isabel T. 'Chomehusvi Shamanism', *Essays in Anthropology*, Berkeley, 1936.

Kern, F. *Der Beginn der Weltgeschichte*, Munich, 1953.

Kirchner, H. 'Ein archäologischer Beitrag zur Urgeschichte des Schamanismus', *Anthropos*, Vol. 47, pp. 244–86, Fribourg, 1952.

Knoll-Greiling, Ursula. 'Beitrag zur Psychologie des Schamanismus bei einigen Völkern des nördlichen Asiens und Amerikas', Inaugural Dissertation, Friedrich-Wilhelms-Universität zu Berlin, Berlin, 1944.

Knoll-Greiling, Ursula. 'Die sozial-psychologische Funktion der Schamenen', *Beiträge zur Gesellungs und Völkerwissenschaft*, Berlin, 1950.

Knoll-Greiling, Ursula. 'Berufung und Berufungserlebnis bei den Schamanen', *Tribus*, Vol. 2/3, pp. 227–38, Stuttgart, 1953.

Knoll-Greiling, Ursula. 'Rauschinduzierende Mittel bei Naturvölkern und ihre individuelle und soziale Wirkung', *Sociologus Neue Folge*, Jg. 9, No. 1, Berlin, 1959.

Knoll-Greiling, Ursula. 'Ähnlichkeit im Verhalten der Schamanen mit der des paroxysmalen Typs der Szondi'schen Triebpsychologie', *Beiträge zur Diagnostik, Prognostik und Therapie des Schicksals*, Bern/Stuttgart, c. 1959.

Koch-Grünberg, Theodor. *Vom Roiroima zum Orinoko*, Berlin, 1916.

Kodolányi jr., J. 'Antal Reguly', *Glaubenswelt und Folklore der sibirischen Völker*, pp. 17–28, Budapest, 1963.

Kodolányi jr., J. 'Speicher der Chanten (Ostjaken) für Opfergegenstände', *Glaubenswelt und Folklore der sibirischen Völker*, pp. 111–14, Budapest, 1963.

Koppers, W. 'Probleme der indischen Religionsgeschichte', *Anthropos*, Vol. 35/63, pp. 761–814, Fribourg, 1940–1.

Kramer, S. N. 'Sumerian Mythology', *Memoirs of the American Philosophical Society*, Vol. 21, Philadelphia, 1944.

Krause, Aruel. *Die Tlinkit-Indianer*, Jena, 1885.

Krauss, F. S. 'Das Schamanenthum der Jakuten', *Mitt. d. Anthropologischen Gesellschaft in Wien*, Vol. 18, pp. 165–82, Vienna, 1888.

Kremsmayer, Helmo. 'Schamanismus und Seelenvorstellung im alten China', *Archiv für Völkerkunde*, Vol. IX, pp. 66–78, Vienna, 1954.

Krickeberg, W. *Indianermärchen aus Nordamerika*, Jena, 1924.

Krickeberg, W. 'Bauform und Weltbild im alten Mexico', *Paideuma*, Vol. 4, pp. 295–333, Bamberg, 1950.

Krickeberg, W. *Altmexikanische Kulturen*, Berlin, 1956.

Kroeber, A. L. 'Preliminary Sketch of the Mohave Indians of California', *American Anthropologist*, Vol. 4, 1902.

Kroeber, A. L. 'The Arapaho', *Amer. Mus. of Nat. Hist. Bull.*, Vol. 18, 1907.

Kroeber, A. L. *The Religion of the Indians of California*, Univ. of California, Publ. in American Archaeology and Ethnology, Vol. 4, No. 6, 1907.

Kroeber, A. L. 'Totem and Taboo, an Ethnologic Psychoanalysis', *American Anthropologist*, Vol. 22, 1920.

Kroll, J. 'Gott und Hölle', *Der Mythos vom Descensuskampfe*, Berlin, 1932.

Ksenofontov, G. V. 'Chrestes. Samanizm i christianstwo' (Chrestes. Schamanismus und Christentum), Irkutsk, 1929.

Ksenofontov, G. V. 'Legendy o šamanach' (Schamanenlegenden), Irkutsk, 1928.

Kühn, H. *Die Felsbilder Europas*, 2. Aufl., Stuttgart, 1952.

Kühn, Herbert. *Eiszeitmalerei*, Munich, 1946.

Lankenau, H. von. 'Die Schamanen und das Schamanenwesen', *Globus*, Vol. 22, pp. 278–83, Braunschweig, 1872.

Laufer, Berthold. 'Origin of the word Shaman', *American Anthropologist*, Vol. 19, 197.

Layard, J. W. 'Shamanism. An Analysis Based on Comparison with the Flying Tricksters of Malekula', *Journal of the Royal Anthroploigical Institute*, Vol. 60, pp. 525–50, London, 1930.

Lehmann, Alfred. *Aberglaube und Zauberei*, Stuttgart, 1898.

Lehmann, Edward. *Mystik im Heidentum und Christentum*, Leipzig, 1908.

Lehtisalo, T. 'Der Tod und die Wiedergeburt des künftigen Schamanen', *Journal de la Société Finno-Ougrienne*, Vol. 48, pp. 1–34, 1937.

Leuba, James. *Die Psychologie der religiösen Mystik*, Munich, 1927.

Levin, M. G.; Potapov, L. P. *Narody Sibiri*, Moskva/Leningrad, 1956.

Lewis, Louis. *Phantastica*, Berlin, 1924.

Lid, Nils. *North European Shamanism, Men and Culture*, pp. 305–8, Philadelphia, 1960.

Lincoln, Jack Steward. *The Dream in Primitive Cultures*, London, 1935.

Lommel, Andreas. 'Die Unambal. Ein Stamm in Nordwest-Australien', *Monographien zur Völkerkunde, herausgegeben vom Hamburgischen Museum für Völkerkunde*, No. II, Hamburg, 1952.

Lommel, Andreas and Katharina. *Die Kunst des fünften Erdteils Australien*, Munich, 1959.

Lopatin, Ivan A. 'A shamanistic performance for a sick boy', *Anthropos*, Vol. 41-44, pp. 365-8, Fribourg, 1946-9.

Lot-Falck, E. *Les rites de chasse chez les peuples sibériens*, Paris, 1953.

Lot-Falck, Eveline. 'Enrichissements du Département des Terres Arctiques', *Objets et Mondes*, I, Fasc. 2, pp. 49-52, Paris, 1961.

Lowie, Robert H. 'The Tobacco Society of the Crow Indians', *Amer. Mus. of Nat. Hist. Anthropological Papers*, Vol. 21, 1919.

Lowie, Robert H. 'The Religion of the Crow Indians', *Amer. Mus. of Nat. Hist. Anthropological Papers*, Vol. 25, Part 2, 1922.

Lowie, Robert H. *Primitive Religion*, New York, 1924.

Lublinsky, Ida. 'Der Medizinmann bei den Naturvölkern Südamerikas', *Zeitschrift f. Ethnologie*, Berlin, 1920.

McKorn, W. C. *Functional Families of the Patwin*. Univ. of California, Publ. in American Archaeology and Ethnology, Vol. 13, 1917-23.

Madsen, W. 'Shamanism in Mexico', *Southwestern Journal of Anthropology*, Vol. II, pp. 48-57, 1955.

Malinowsky, Bronislaw, *The Sexual Life of Savages in North-West Melanesia*, London, 1929.

Mándoki, L. 'Asiatische Sternnamen', *Glaubenswelt und Folklore der sibirischen Völker*, pp. 519-32, Budapest, 1963.

Manker, Ernst. *Die lappische Zaubertrommel*, Stockholm, 1938.

Manker, E. 'Seite-Kult und Trommelmagie der Lappen', *Glaubenswelt und Folklore der sibirischen Völker*, pp. 29-43, Budapest, 1963.

Manker, E. 'The Noaidde Art', *Folk*, Vol. 5, pp. 235-44, Copenhagen, 1963.

Marót, K. 'Vallás és mágia', *Ethnographia*, Vol. 44, pp. 31-44; Vol. 45, pp. 81-83, 1933-4.

Matjustichenko, W. I. 'Zur Kunst der alten Stämme an der Mündung des Tom', *Glaubenswelt und Folklore der sibirischen Völker*, pp. 513-18, Budapest, 1963.

Matthews, Wash. *The Mountain Chant*, Bureau of American Ethnology, Annual Reports, Vol. V, 1887.

Melnikow, N. 'Die ehemal. Menschenopfer und der Schamanismus bei den Burjaten des Irkutskschen Gouvernements', *Globus*, 75, pp. 132-4.

Menowstschikow, G. A. 'Wissen, religiöse Vorstellungen und Riten der asiatischen Eskimos', *Glaubenswelt und Folklore der sibirischen Völker*, pp. 463-81, Budapest, 1963.

Métraux, A. *Religion and Shamanism, Handbook of South American Indians*, Vol. 5, Smithsonian Institution, Bureau of American Ethnology, Bulletin 143, Washington, 1949.

Meuli, K. 'Scythica', *Hermes*, Vol. 70, pp. 121-76, 1935.

Meuli, K. 'Griechische Opferbräuche, Phyllobolia für Peter von der Mühll zum 60', *Geburtstag*, pp. 185-288, Basle, 1946.

Mikhailovskii, V. M. 'Shamanism in Siberia and European Russia', *Journ. of the Anthr. Inst. of Great Britain and Ireland*, Vol. XXIV, pp. 62-100, 126-58, London, 1895.

Mooney, James. *The Ghost Dance Religion and the Sioux Outbreak of 1890*, Bureau of American Ethnology, Annual Reports, Vol. 14, Washington, 1896.

Moschinskaja, W. 'Über einige alte anthropomorphe Darstellungen aus Westsibirien', *Glaubenswelt und Folklore der sibirischen Völker*, pp. 101-10, Budapest, 1963.

Mühlmann, W. E. 'Hyperboräische Eschatologie', *Chiliasmus und Nativismus*, pp. 197-221, Berlin, 1961.

Muster, W. *Der Schamanismus und seine Spuren in der Saga, im deutschen Brauch, Märchen und Glauben*. Diss. Graz, 1947. Review: *Deutsches Jahrb. f. Volkskunde*, Vol. 2, pp. 231-2, 1956.

Muster, W. *Der Schamanismus bei den Etruskern, Frühgeschichte und Sprachwissenschaft*, pp. 60-77, Vienna, 1948.

Nachtigall, H. 'Die kulturhistorische Wurzel der Schamanenskelettierung', *Zeitschrift für Ethnologie*, Vol. 77, pp. 188-97, Braunschweig, 1952.

Nachtigall, H. 'Die erhöhte Bestattung in Nord- und Hochasien', *Anthropos*, Vol. 48, pp. 44-70, Fribourg, 1953.

Nachtigall, H. 'Schamanismus bei den Paez-Indianern', *Zeitschrift für Ethnologie*, Vol. 78, pp. 210-23, Braunschweig, 1953.

Nahodil, O. 'Mutterkult in Sibirien', *Glaubenswelt und Folklore der sibirischen Völker*, pp. 491-511, Budapest, 1963.

Narr, K. J. *Hirten, Pflanzer, Bauern: Produktionsstufe, Historia Mundi*, Vol. 2, pp. 66-100, Munich, 1953.

Narr, K. J. 'Nordasiatisch-europäische Urzeit in archäologischer und völkerkundlicher Sicht', Studium Generale, Vol. 7, pp. 193–210, 1954.

Narr, K. J. Vorderasien, Nordafrika und Europa, Abriß der Vorgeschichte, pp. 1–84, Munich, 1957.

Narr, K. J. Bärenzeremoniell und Schamanismus in der Älteren Steinzeit Europas, Saeculum, Vol. X, pp. 233–72, Freiburg and Munich, 1959.

Nelson, E. W. The Eskimos about Bering-street, Bureau of American Ethnology, Annual Reports, Vol. 18, Washington, 1896.

Nieuwenhuis, Anton Willem. Grundbegriffe der Magie und ihre psychologische Bedeutung, 21, Internat. Americ. Congress, 1924.

Nioradze, Georg. Der Schamanismus bei den sibirischen Völkern, Stuttgart, 1925.

Nölle, W. 'Schamanistische Vorstellungen im Shaktismus', Jahrb. d. Mus. f. Völkerkunde zu Leipzig, Vol. II, pp. 41–47, Leipzig, 1952.

Nölle, W. 'Iranisch-nordostasiatische Beziehungen im Schamanismus', Jahrb. d. Mus. f. Völkerkunde zu Leipzig, Vol. 12, pp. 86–90, 1953, Leipzig, 1954.

Norden, E. P. Vergilius Maro Aeneis Buch, VI (4. Aufl.), Darmstadt, 1957.

Nyberg, H. S. Die Religionen des alten Iran, Leipzig, 1938.

Obermaier, H. Der Mensch der Vorzeit, Berlin/Munich/Vienna, 1912.

Ohlmarks, Ake. Studien zum Problem des Schamanismus, London and Copenhagen, 1939.

Okladnikov, A. P. 'Drevnie šamanskie izobraženija iz Vostočnoj Sibiri', Sovetskaja Archeologija, Vol. 10, pp. 203–25, 1948.

Okladnikov, A. P. 'Neolit i bronzovyj vek Pribajkalja, III', Materialy i Issledovanija po Archeologii S.S.S.R., No. 43, Moskva/Leningrad, 1955.

Pallas, Petrus Simon. Reise durch verschiedene Provinzen des russischen Reiches, St Petersburg, 1771–6.

Park, Willard, Z. Shamanism in Western North America, Northwestern University, Evanston and Chicago, 1938.

Park, Willard, Z. 'Paviotso Shamanism', American Anthropologist, Vol. 36, 1934.

Paulson, Hultkrantz Jettmar. Die Religion Nordeurasiens und die amerikanische Arktis, Stuttgart, 1962.

Paulson, Ivar. Die primitiven Seelenvorstellungen der nordeurasischen Völker. The Ethnographical Museum of Sweden, Monograph Series—Publication No. 5, Stockholm, 1958.

Paulson, Ivar. 'Die Schutzgeister und Gottheiten der Jagdtiere im Glauben der nordasiatischen (sibirischen) Völker', Zeitschrift für Ethnologie, Vol. 85, pp. 82–117, Braunschweig, 1960.

Paulson, Ivar. 'Seelenvorstellungen und Totenglaube bei nordeurasischen Völkern', Ethnos, 1960, pp. 84–118, Stockholm, 1960.

Paulson, I. 'Zur Aufbewahrung der Tierknochen im Jagdritual der nordeurasischen Völker', Glaubenswelt und Folklore der sibirischen Völker, pp. 483–90, Budapest, 1963.

Pechüel-Loesche, Eduard. Die Loango-Expedition, 1873. Leipzig, 1897.

Perrot, N. Les représentations de l'arbre sacré sur les monuments de Mésopotamie et d'Elam, Paris, 1937.

Petri, Helmut. 'Der Australische Medizinmann', Annali Lateranensi, Vol. XVI, pp. 159–317; XVII, pp. 157–225, Vatican City, 1952 and 1953.

Pettersson, O. 'Jabmek and Jabmeaimo. A Comparative Study of the Dead and the Realm of the Dead in Lappish Religion', Lunds Universitets Arsskrft, N.F. Avd. I, Vol. 52, No. 6, Lund, 1957.

Pf. L. 'Der Arzt in der vorkolumbischen Zeit. Korresp. Blätter d. Allg. ärztlich', Vereins von Thüringen, No. 11, 1919.

Pilsudski, B. 'Der Schamanismus bei den Ainu-Stämmen von Sahalin', Globus, 95, pp. 72–78.

Popon, A. A. Materialy dija bibliografii russkoj literatury po izučeniju šamanstva severoaziatskich narodov. Leningrad, 1932.

Popow, A. A. 'Wie Sereptie D'aruoskin zum Schamanen erwählt wurde', Glaubenswelt und Folklore der sibirischen Völker, pp. 149–59, Budapest, 1963.

Potapow, L. P. 'Die Schamanentrommel bei den altaischen Völkerschaften', Glaubenswelt und Folklore der sibirischen Völker, pp. 223–56, Budapest, 1963.

Potratz, H. 'Bär und Hase in der Bildkunst des alten Luristan', Archiv. für Orientforschung, Vol. 17, pp. 121–88, 1954–6.

Preuss, Konrad Theodor. Die Eingeborenen Amerikas, Tübingen, 1926.

Priklonsky, V. L. 'Das Schamanentum der Yakuten', Mitt. d. Wiener anthr. Ges., Vol. 18, Vienna, 1888.

Prokofyeva, Ye. D. 'The Costume of an Enets Shaman', *Studies in Siberian Shamanism*, pp. 124–56, Toronto, 1963.

Prümm, K. *Religionsgeschichtliches Handbuch für den Raum der altchristlichen Umwelt*, Rome, 1954.

Radin, Paul. 'The Ritual and Significance of the Winnebago Medicine Dance', *Journal of American Folk-Lore*, Vol. 24, 1911.

Radin, Paul, 'A Sketch of the Peyote Cult of the Winnebago. Study in Borrowing', *Journal of Religious Psychology*, Vol. 7, 1914.

Radin, Paul. *The Autobiography of a Winnebago Indian*. Univ. of California, Publ. in American Archaeology and Ethnology, Vol. 16, 1920.

Radin, Paul. *Primitive Man as Philosopher*, New York, 1927.

Radloff, Wilhelm. *Aus Sibirien*. Leipzig, 1884.

Rahmann, Rudolf. 'Shamanistic and related phenomena in Northern and Middle India', *Anthropos*, Vol. 54, pp. 681–760, Fribourg, 1959.

Rasmussen, Knud. *Grönlandsagen*, Berlin, 1922.

Rasmussen, Knud. *Thulefahrt*, Frankfurt, 1925.

Riemschneider, M. *Der Wettergott*, Leipzig, 1956.

Rock, J. F. 'Contributions to the Shamanism of the Tibetan-Chinese Borderland', *Anthropos*, Vol. 54, pp. 796–181, Fribourg, 1959.

Röder, J. 'Pfahl und Menhir', *Studien zur westeuropäischen Altertumskunde*, Vol. 1, Neuwied, 1949.

Róheim, G. 'Hungarian and Vogul Mythology', *Monographs of the American Ethnological Society*, Vol. 23, Locust Valley, New York, 1954.

Rombandjejewa, E. I. 'Einige Sitten und Bräuche der Mansen (Wogulen) bei der Geburt der Kinder', *Glaubenswelt und Folklore der sibirischen Völker*, pp. 85–92, Budapest, 1963.

Roux, Jean-Paul. 'Eléments chamaniques dans les textes prémongols', *Anthropos*, Vol. 53, pp. 441–56, Fribourg, 1958.

Roux, Jean-Paul. 'Le nom du chaman dans les textes turcomongols', *Anthropos*, Vol. 53, pp. 133–42, Fribourg, 1958.

Roux, Jean-Paul. 'Le chaman gingiskhanide', *Anthropos*, Vol. 54, pp. 401–31, Fribourg, 1959.

Roux, J. P. 'Le chaman altaique d'après les voyageurs européens des XVIIe et XVIIIe siècles', *Anthropos*, Vol. 56, pp. 438–58, Fribourg, 1961.

Ruben, W. 'Schamanismus im alten Indien', *Acta Orientalia*, Vol. 17, pp. 164–205, 1939.

Ruben, W. *Die Philosophie der Upanishaden*, Berlin, 1947.

Ruben, W. *Einführung in die Indienkunde*, Berlin, 1954.

Rudenko, C. I. 'Grafičkoe iskusstvo ostjakov i vogulov', *Materialy po etnografii*, Vol. IV, pp. 13–40, Etnografi-českij otdel gocudarst-vennogo russkogo muzeja, Leningrad, 1929.

Russell, Frank. *The Pima Indians*, Bureau of American Ethnology, Annual Reports, Vol. 25, 1908.

Sadnik, L. 'Der Balkan und die Hochkulturen des Vorderen Orients', *Saeculum*, Vol. 5, pp. 34–40, Freiburg/Munich, 1954.

Samoywassow, Isw. *Wost. sib. Otd. Rossk. Geogr. Abachtsch, I*, XVII, Irkutsk, 1886.

Sandin, Benedict. 'Salang changed his sex', *Sarawak Mus. Journ.*, Vol. VIII, 10/25, pp. 145–52, Kuching, 1957.

Sandschejew, Garma. 'Weltanschauung und Schamanismus der Alaren-Burjaten', *Anthropos*, Vol. 22, pp. 576–613, 933–55; Vol. 23, pp. 538–60, 967–86, Mödling b. Vienna, 1927–8.

Sapir, Edward. 'Religious Ideas of the Takelma Indians of Southwestern Oregon', *Journal of American Folk-Lore*, Vol. 20, 1907.

Schilder, Paul. *Wahn und Erkenntnis*, Berlin, 1918.

Schirokogorow (Širokogorov) S. M. 'Versuch einer Erforschung der Grundlagen des Schamanentums bei den Tungusen', *Baessler Archiv*, Vol. XVIII, pp. 41–96, Berlin, 1935.

Schmidt, M. 'Die materielle Wirtschaft bei den Naturvölkern', *Wissenschaft und Bildung*, Vol. 185, Leipzig, 1925.

Schmidt, P. W. *Der Ursprung der Gottesidee*, Vol. III, IX–XII, Münster i. W., 1931, 1949–55.

Schmidt, P. W. *Handbuch der Methode der kulturhistorischen Ethnologie*, Münster i. W., 1937.

Schmidt, P. W. 'Untersuchungen zur Methode der Ethnologie', *Anthropos*, Vol. 35/36, pp. 898–965, 1940–1.

Schmidt, P. W. 'Die Urkulturen: Ältere Jagd- und Sammelstufe', *Historia Mundi*, Vol. I, pp. 375–501, Munich, 1952.

Schmidt, R. R. *Der Geist der Vorzeit*, Berlin, 1934.

Schmücker, Aenne. *Die große Schlittenreise*, Düsseldorf, 1946.

Schmücker, Aenne. *Schneehüttenlieder*, Essen, 1947.

Schneider, Karl. *Die Psychologie der Schizophrenen und ihre Bedeutung für die Klinik der Schizophrenie*, Leipzig, 1930.

Schorsch, Gerhard. *Zur Theorie der Halluzinationen*, Leipzig, 1934.

Schram, L. M. J. 'The Monguors of the Kansu-Tibetan Border. Part II: Their Religious Life', *Transactions of the American Philosophical Society*, N. S., Vol. 47, Part I, Philadelphia, 1957.

Schramm, P. E. 'Herrschaftszeichen und Staatssymboli, Vol. I: Monumenta Germaniae Historica', *Schriften*, Vol. 13/1, Stuttgart, 1954.

Schröder, D. 'Das Herbst-Dankopfer der T'ujen im Sining-Gabiet, Nordwest-China', *Anthropos*, Vol. 37/40, pp. 867–73, Fribourg, 1942–5.

Schröder, D. 'Rezension: M. Eliade, Le Chamanisme et les Techniques archaiques de l'extase', *Anthropos*, Vol. 48, pp. 671–8, Fribourg, 1953.

Schröder, Dominik. 'Zur Struktur des Schamanismus', *Anthropos*, Vol. 50, pp. 848–81, Fribourg, 1955.

Schultz, Johann Heinrich. 'Über Schichtenbildung im hypnotischen Selbstbeachten', *Monatszeitschrift für Psychiatrie und Neurologie*, 1921.

Schultz, Johann Heinrich. *Das autogene Training*, Leipzig, 1934.

Schuster, Meinhard. 'Die Schamanen und ihr Ritual: Burghard Freudenfeld', *Völkerkunde*, Munich, 1960.

Sieroszewsky, Waclaw. *Zwölf Jahre im Lande der Yakuten*, Warsaw, 1935.

Shimkin, B. D. 'A Sketch of the Ket, or Yenissei Ostyak', *Ethnos*, Vol. 4, pp. 147–76, Stockholm, 1939.

Siiger, H. 'Shamanism among the Kalash Kafirs of Chitral', *Folk*, Vol. 5, pp. 295–303, Copenhagen, 1963.

Skeat, Walter William. *Malay Magic*, London, 1900.

Skinner, Alanson. 'Social Life and Ceremonial Bundles of the Indians', *Amer. Mus. of Nat. Hist. Anthropological Papers*, Vol. XIII, 1913.

Smith, Marian W. 'Shamanism in the Shaker Religion of Northwest America', *Man*, Vol. 54, Art. 181, pp. 119–22, London, 1954.

Soden, W. von. *Neue Bände der 'Archives de Mâri' Orientalia*, Vol. 22, pp. 193–209, 1953.

Söderblom, Nathan. *Om makten och själen*, Vorwort zu: Stadling, J: Shamanismen i norra Asien, Stockholm, 1912.

Spier, Leslie. 'The Prophet Dance of the Northwest and its Derivatives: The Source of the Ghost Dance', *General Series in Anthropology*, I, New Haven, 1935.

Spier, Leslie. *Klamath Ethnography*, Univ. of California, Publ. in American Archaeology and Ethnology, Vol. 30, 1930.

Spiess, K. 'Neue Marksteine', *Veröffentlichungen des Österreichischen Museums für Volkskunde*, Vol. 7, Vienna, 1955.

Stadling, J. 'Shamanismen i norra Asien', *Populära etnologiska skrifter*, 7, Stockholm, 1912.

Staudemaier, L. *Die Magie als experimentelle Naturwissenschaft*, Leipzig, 1912.

Steinitz, W. 'Ein ostjakisches Märchen in M. A. Castréns handschriftlichem Nachlaß', *Glaubenswelt und Folklore der sibirischen Völker*, pp. 114–19, Budapest, 1963.

Stell, Otto. *Suggestion und Hypnotismus in der Völkerkunde*, Leipzig, 1894.

Sternberg, Leo. 'Divine Election in Primitive Religion', *Proceedings of the 21st International Congress of America*, pp. 472–512, Göteborg, 1925.

Sternberg, L. 'Der Adlerkult bei den Völkern Sibiriens', *Archiv für Religionswissenschaft*, Vol. 28, pp. 125–53, 1930.

Stieda, L. 'Das Schamanentum unter den Burjäten', *Globus*, Vol. LII, pp. 250–3, 268–70, 286–8, 299–301, 316–18, Braunschweig, 1887.

Stiglmayr, Engelbert, 'Schamanismus der Negrito Südostasiens', *Wiener Völkerkundliche Mitteilungen*, Vol. 2, pp. 156–64; Vol. 3, pp. 14–20; Vol. 4, pp. 135–46, Vienna, 1954–6.

Stiglmayr, E. 'Schamanismus in Polynesien' (Diss. Excerpt), *Wiener Völkerkundliche Mitteilungen*, Vol. 4, pp. 85–88, Vienna, 1956.

Stiglmayr, E. 'Schamanismus in Australien', *Wiener Völkerkundliche Mitteilungen*, Vol. 5, pp. 161–90, Vienna, 1957.

Stiglmayr, E. 'Schamanismus, eine spirituelische Religion?' *Ethnos*, Vol. 27, pp. 40–48, Stockholm, 1962.

Storch, Alfred. *Das archaisch-primitive Erleben und Denken der Schizophrenen*, Berlin, 1922.

Straube, H. 'Die Tierverkleidungen der afrikanischen Naturvölker', *Studien zur Kulturkunde*, Vol. 13, Wiesbaden, 1955.

Swanton, John Reed. *The Haida of Queen Charlotte Island*, Jesup North Pacific Expedition, Leiden, 1905.

Sydow, Eckart von. *Kunst und Religion der Naturvölker*, Oldenburg, 1926.

Taksami, Tsch. M. 'Zu den alten religiösen Riten und Verboten der Nivchen (Giljaken)', *Glaubenswelt und Folklore der sibirischen Völker*, pp. 437–52, Budapest, 1963.

Teit, James. 'The Thompson Indians of British Columbia', *Amer. Mus. of Nat. Hist. Memoirs*, Vol. 12, Part 4, 1900.

Teit, James. 'The Lilooet Indians', *Amer. Mus. of Nat. Hist. Memoirs*, Vol. 14, Part 5, 1909.

Thalbitzer, Williams. 'Les Magiciens Esquimaux', *Journal de la Société des Americanistes*, N. S., Vol. XXII, Paris, 1930.

Thurnwald, Hilde. 'Die schwarze Frau im Wandel Afrikas', *Forschungen zur Völkerpsychologie u. Soziologie*, Stuttgart, 1935.

Thurnwald, Hilde. *Menschen der Südsee*, Stuttgart, 1937.

Thurnwald, Richard. *Forschungen auf den Salomo-Inseln und dem Bismarck-Archipel*, Berlin, 1912.

Thurnwald, Richard. 'Ethno-psychologische Studien auf dem Bismarck-Archipel und den Salomo-Inseln', *Zeitschrift für angewandte Psychologie*, Reihe 6, Leipzig, 1913.

Thurnwald, Richard. 'Rausch', *Reallexikon für Vorgeschichte*, 1914.

Thurnwald, Richard. 'Die Psychologie des Totemismus', *Anthropos*, XII–XIII, pp. 1094–1113; XIV–XV, pp. 496, Mödling b. Vienna, 1917–20.

Thurnwald, Richard. *Entstehung von Staat und Familie*, Mannheim, 1921.

Thurnwald, Richard. 'Psychologie des primitiven Menschen', *Handbuch für angewandte Psychologie*, 1922.

Thurnwald, Richard. 'Die Eingeborenen Australiens und der Südseeinseln', *Religionsgeschichtl. Lesebuch*, 2. Aufl., Heft 8, Tübingen, 1927.

Thurnwald, Richard. 'Grundprobleme der vergleichenden Völkerpsychologie', *Zeitschrift für die ges. Staatswissenschaft* 87/2, Tübingen, 1929.

Thurnwald, Richard. 'Die menschliche Gesellschaft in ihren ethnosoziologischen Grundlagen. Bd. I', *Repräsentative Lebensbilder von Naturvölkern*, Berlin, 1931.

Thurnwald, Richard. *Werden, Wandel und Gestaltung der Wirtschaft*, 1932.

Thurnwald, Richard. *Werden, Wandel und Gestaltung von Familie, Verwandtschaft und Bünden*, 1932.

Thurnwald, Richard. *Werden, Wandel und Gestaltung des Rechts im Lichte der Völkerforschung*, 1934.

Thurnwald, Richard. *Black and White in East Africa*, London, 1935.

Thurnwald, Richard. *Werden, Wandel und Gestaltung von Staat und Kultur*, 1935.

Thurnwald, Richard. *Primitive Initiations-und Wiedergeburtsriten*. Eranos-Jahrbuch, Zürich, 1940.

Tokarev, S. *Šamanstvo, ili šamanizm. Bolšaja Svetskaja Enciklopedija*, Vol. 61, pp. 802–3, 1934.

Torginetz. 'Aus dem Leben der Sibirischen Eingeborenen', *Sibir*, No. 18, April 1883.

Troshansky, Vasily Pilipporio. *Skizzen über d. Jakuten des Bezirks Jakutsk*, Kazan, 1918.

Vajda, László. 'Zur phaseologischen Stellung des Schamanismus', *Ural-Altaische Jahrbücher*, Vol. XXXI, pp. 456–85, Wiesbaden, 1959.

Vanoverbergh, Morice. 'Religion and Magic among the Isneg', *Anthropos*, Vol. 48, pp. 71–104, 557–68; Vol. 49, pp. 4–12; Vol. 50, pp. 212–40, Fribourg, 1953–5.

Vasilevich, G. M. 'Early Concepts about the Universe Among the Evenks (Material)', *Studies in Siberian Shamanism*, pp. 46–83, Toronto, 1963.

Vasiljev, V. N. 'Description d'un costume et d'un tabourin de Chaman chez les Jakuts (Russian)', *Publications du Musée d'Anthrop. et d'ethnogr. de l'Acad. de Petersburg*, VIII, St Petersburg, 1910.

Vértes, E. 'Auf der Spur mythischer Gesänge der Ostjaken', *Glaubenswelt und Folklore der sibirischen Völker*, pp. 121–30, Budapest, 1963.

Viennot, O. *Le culte de l'arbre dans l'Inde ancienne*, Paris, 1954.

Vierkant, A. *Selbsterhaltung der religiösen Systemen*, *Vierteljahrsschrift für wissenschaftliche Philosophie und Soziologie*, Vol. XXIV, Leipzig, 1902.

Wagner, Günter. 'Die Religion der Bantu von Kavirondo', *Zeitschrift für Ethnologie*, Vol. 71, pp. 201–19, Berlin, 1940.

Wales, H. G. Q. *The Mountain of God*, London, 1953.

Waley, Arthur. *The Nine Songs: A Study of Shamanism in Ancient China*, London, 1955.

Wasiljew, Victor. 'Ein tungusisches Schamanengrab', *Globus*, Vol. 96, pp. 314–17, Braunschweig, 1909.

Wassén, H. 'An Analogy between a South American and Oceanic Myth Motif and Negro Influence in Darien', *Etnologiska Studier*, Vol. 10, pp. 69–79, Göteborg, 1940.

Wassiljewitsch, G. M. 'Erwerbung der Schamanenfähigkeiten bei den Ewenken (Tungusen)', *Glaubenswelt und Folklore der sibirischen Völker*, pp. 369–80, Budapest, 1963.

Wassiljewitsch, G. M. 'Schamanengesänge der Ewenken (Tungusen)', *Glaubenswelt und Folklore der sibirischen Völker*, pp. 381–404, Budapest, 1963.

Waterbury, Florence. 'Bird-Deities in China', *Artibus Asiae*, Supplement X, Ascona, 1952.

Weinstein, S. I. 'Die Schamanentrommel der Tuwa u. die Zeremonie ihrer "Belebung"', *Glaubenswelt und Folklore der sibirischen Völker*, pp. 359–67, Budapest, 1963.

Weisweiler, J. 'Die Kultur der irischen Heldensage', *Paideuma*, Vol. 4, pp. 149–70, Wiesbaden, 1950.

Werbow, G. D. 'Bestattungsriten bei den Enzen (Jenissei-Samojeden)', *Glaubenswelt und Folklore der sibirischen Völker*, pp. 131–3, Budapest, 1963.

Werner, J. 'Beiträge zur Archäologie des Attila-Reiches', *Bayer. Akad. d. Wiss., Phil.-hist. Klasse, Abhandlungen*, N.F., H. 38, Munich, 1956.

Wilbert, Johannes. 'Dijubos de indios venezolanos 48 obras originales de las tribus Sanema o Shirishana y Warao', *Antropológica*, No. 11, pp. 30–60, Caracas, 1962.

Winstedt, R. O. *The Malay Magician being Shaman, Saiva and Sufi*. London, 1961.

Wissler, Clark. *Mythology of the Blackfoot Indians, Amer. Mus. of Nat. Hist. Anthropological Papers*, Vol. II, 1909.

Wolfram, R. 'Robin Hood and Hobby Horse', *Wiener Prähistorische Zeitschrift*, Vol. 19, pp. 357–74, Vienna, 1932.

Zelenin, D. 'Ein erotischer Ritus in den Opferungen der altaischen Türken', *Internat. Arch. f. Ethnographie*, Vol. 29, pp. 83–98, 1928.

Zelenin, D. M. 'Die animistische Philosophie des sibirischen Schamanismus', *Ethnos*, I, 3, pp. 81–85, Stockholm, 1936.

Zelenin, D. K. 'Kult ongonov v Sibiri. Perežitki totemizma v ideologii sibirskich narodov' (The Ongon cult in Siberia. A relic of Totemism in the Ideology of the Siberian Peoples), Trudy Instituta Antropologii, Archeologii i Etnografii (Works of the Inst. f. Anthropology, Archäology and Ethnographic Series), No. 3. Academy of Sciences of the U.S.S.R., Moscow/Leningrad, 1936, 436 pp. with 84 figs.

Zélénine, D. *Le culte des idoles en Sibérie*, Paris, 1952.

Zerries, Otto. *Krankheitsdämonen und Hilfsgeister des Medizinmannes in Südamerika*, Cambridge, 1952.

Zerries, Otto. 'Krankheitsdämonen und Hilfsgeister des Medizinmannes in Südamerika', *Proceedings of the Thirtieth International Congress of Americanists*, pp. 162, 1954.

Zerries, Otto. 'Wild- und Buschgeister in Südamerika', *Studien zur Kulturkunde*, Vol. II, Wiesbaden, 1954.

Zucker, Konrad. 'Psychologie des Schamanisierens', *Zeitschrift für die ges. Neurologie u. Psychiatrie*, Vol. 150, Berlin, 1934.